Religious
Worlds

Religious Worlds

The Comparative Study
of Religion

William E. Paden

Beacon Press
Boston

Beacon Press
25 Beacon Street
Boston, Massachusetts 02108

Beacon Press books
are published under the auspices of
the Unitarian Universalist Association of Congregations.

95 94 93 92 91 90 89   2 3 4 5 6 7 8

Text design by Hunter Graphics

Library of Congress Cataloging-in-Publication Data
Paden, William E.
Religious worlds.
Includes index.
1. Religion. I. Title.
BL48.P22 1988   291   88-47658
ISBN 0-8070-1210-6
ISBN 0-8070-1211-4 (pbk.)

Contents

Preface

More information about religion is available today than ever before, yet our resources for understanding it have hardly kept pace. Even the liberally educated person is equipped with few comparative categories that are genuinely transcultural in their explanatory and descriptive power. Although good texts on the history of the various religious traditions are abundant, books that deal synoptically and thematically with the general cross-cultural patterns of religious life are scarce.

What follows is not a text about different world religions but a *framework* for understanding commonality and diversity among all religious worlds. Central to the book is the theme that religious systems are more effectively understood as "worlds" than as "beliefs," and that these worlds are embodied in the languages of myth, ritual, and other expressive forms. It is an approach that complements rather than competes with historical investigations of religious traditions.

It was not too long ago in American colleges that religion courses consisted simply of instruction in the scriptures, doctrines, and history of Christianity. Gradually offerings on "the non-Christian religions of the world" were added to the curriculum, and then, in the 1960s and independent of any organizational connection with the Judeo-Christian traditions, many universities began to teach the comparative study of religion. The subject matter took its place alongside the other humanities in public universities.

This book focuses ideas and material developed from teaching comparative religion over the last two decades at the University of Vermont. The setting of secular, liberal arts education, with no sectarian assumptions, forced me to think through the themes of this book from the ground up. What sort of thing is a religion? What are the patterns common to all of them? As moderns, what interpretive horizons are available to us? What does it mean to "understand" religion? With what methods should we approach this extraordinary subject matter? I have assumed from the start that any answers to these questions must be derived not just from a parochial field of Western traditions but from the rich diversity of world history.

For their valuable help with drafts of this material, special thanks go to my colleagues Luther H. Martin, Allan A. Andrews, and Robert E. Gussner, and to my wife, Natasha.

Introduction

Comparative Perspective and the Study of Religion

In its elementary sense, comparative religion involves the study of the many religious traditions of the world. Such knowledge about "others" is deprovincializing. But it is one of the purposes of this book to show that the study of religion is not just limited to the description of various religious traditions, as if these were so many belief systems that posed alternatives to one's own or so many objects of intrinsic curiosity. Full comparative perspective involves more than simply describing side by side or serially the religions of the world, as though one were just sampling or judging various claims to truth.

There is also a second dimension of comparative investigation in religion: the study not just of different *religions* but of the structures of *religion*.[1] What do we learn from the many species of religion about the genus itself? Religions do have things in common. They are instances of a human activity that has typical, expressive forms of its own. These religious structures constitute a subject matter in their own right. Like the study of music, which is not limited to examining a sequence of composers but also considers the special world of musical categories such as rhythm and harmony, so the study of religion is not limited to analyzing historical traditions such as Buddhism, Judaism, and Christianity but also investigates the religious "language" common to all traditions, the language of myth, gods, ritual, and sacrifice—in short, the language of "the sacred."

The general categories of religious behavior and the framework they provide for understanding particular religious systems are the primary subject matter of this book. This study therefore addresses the need to go beyond interpreting other religions simply in terms of their relationship to one's own.

1

Dissatisfied with the imposition of European and biblical classifications onto the interpretation of non-Western religious cultures, and eschewing grand, evolutionary hypotheses that simply reflected Western values, modern anthropology understandably abandoned attempts to find overarching patterns in religion and instead devoted itself to in-depth studies of individual cultures. Comparative typologies and concepts are still perceived by many scholars as a dangerously antihistorical endeavor that overlooks the important contexts and particularity of religious symbols and behavior. Certainly comparison has served as a vehicle for all kinds of distortions and apologetics.

Comparison has also been used as a polemical weapon by religions themselves to show the inferiority of other traditions and the superiority of one's own. It has been used to show that all religions are really the same. It has been used to show that all religions are false. Many people sense that the absoluteness of their own beliefs is threatened by the existence of parallels elsewhere. So there is a kind of politics of comparison.

In some ways comparison is simply unavoidable. We all employ comparison every day, and thinking itself is in large measure based on it. It is built into language and perception. What a thing "is" is determined by its similarity and difference with other things like or unlike it. Science would be impossible without it, and without it the realm of metaphor would vanish. The analogical process is part of the way every cultural system classifies its world.

Comparison can create error and distortion as well as insight and knowledge, and this is noticeably so in the area of religion. Religious phenomena have been compared for centuries, but not necessarily in the pursuit of fair description or accurate understanding. Comparison is most often a function of self-interest. It gets used to illustrate one's own ideology. It easily becomes an instrument of judgment, a device for approval or condemnation.

We all tend naturally to reduce areas of life to certain themes that fit our own worldview. As we thematize our world so we thematize religion. Everyone has summarizing ideas, usually positive or negative in connotation, about religion, and religious phenomena become occasions for all manner of precritical impressionistic generalizations. Thus, religion is "about" love, money, God, social repression, escapism. All sects become "systems of brainwashing," oriental religions are "navel gazing." These approaches reduce religious phenomena to imagined stereotypes and ignore all evidence inconsistent with the type. It is as if the mind innately needs to reduce and typify experience in order to avoid the confusion and contradiction that might come with confronting religious diversity. The issue, then, is not *whether* to generalize and thematize about religion, but *how* to do so in appropriate and accurate ways.

In spite of the potential dangers of misuse, comparative perspective is a necessity for any field of study, and without it no real understanding of religion is possible. In this book I have tried to lay out a conceptual framework that avoids some of the past difficulties with comparative biases while still resolutely maintaining the importance and application of cross-cultural categories. Let us consider at the outset a summary of how the concept "comparative perspective" will be used.

1. First and most broadly, comparative perspective is not just a matter of juxtaposing one religion with another, but is the process of understanding any continuities and differences in the history of all types of religious phenomena. Comparative perspective is the knowledge of the whole in relation to the part, which are mutually informative. Every field of knowledge has its equivalent framework. Comparative literature, for example, studies not just writings other than English but themes, genres, and topics common to the whole history of literature as a human enterprise.

2. Comparative perspective is derived inductively from historical knowledge, not deductively from one's own philosophy. Comparative study presupposes history. It is not an alternative to historical perspective but an enrichment of it. Every religious expression has its own unique context of meaning, its own distinctive configuration that is different in some way from others. Historical facts keep typologies honest, testing and challenging comparative generalizations at every point.

3. Comparative perspective involves different levels of specificity, different levels of part-to-whole relationship. One

can compare what a certain pilgrimage means to all people at one time and place, or one can compare that pilgrimage with all others within the same religion, or one can study pilgrimage as a theme that is manifest in all times and religions. Although this particular book makes a point of focusing on transcultural religious forms of the broadest generic scope, many "types" of religious expression—such as saviors, priests, or temples—are not found universally but within certain regions, periods, or types of religion. Much specific comparative work is best limited to studies of variations within a single religious culture or cluster of cultures. Each kind of phenomenon researched will have its own justifiable scope of comparative data and analysis.

4. Where comparative analysis deals with similarity, it deals with analogy rather than with identity,[2] in which things, otherwise unlike, are similar in some respects. It is not just a matter of identifying what is "the same" everywhere. The *significance* of the analogies or parallels is a matter of judgment.

5. Comparative work is not only a process of establishing similarities or analogies. It is also the fundamental instrument for discerning differences. The point needs stressing because this double function has not been fully appreciated. Many people fear that comparative approaches lose sight of the richness of cultural diversity. But the study of continuity (or parallels) and the study of individuality cannot be separated. Only by seeing what is common between things can one see what is different or innovative about any one of them. A Christian or Jewish theology cannot fully understand its own uniqueness and its nuances, without knowing which of its features belong to religion in general and which are distinctively its own.

6. Finally, comparison is not an end in itself. It yields comparative *perspective*, the process by which overarching themes on the one hand and historical particulars on the other get enriched by the way they illumine each other. Because it is the central purpose of this book to illustrate this larger process, let us consider it a little further here.

There is a creative interplay between structure and example that enriches understanding of both. The variations develop, reveal, "work" the theme, as does a set of musical variations. Or, shifting the analogy, the species add to our understanding of the genus, just as the genus calls attention

to common patterns present in a species. Many different creatures—such as fish, birds, mammals—amplify the theme "ver-
tebrate." Dolphins, giraffes, armadillos, and humans are
interestingly different versions of what a mammal can be. One
could say the same of any theme or subject: bicycles and jets
show what transportation can be, pianos and flutes demonstrate what musical instruments can be, Gandhi and Napoleon
embody what leadership can be.

It is exactly the same with religious forms. Our understanding of what religious language and practice "can be" is
diminished if we do not have the most complete awareness of
its possible variations. By looking at all the gods in religious
history, we see more fully what a god is. The variations make
the theme stronger and more interesting. By seeing all the
different things observed in various rites, we see more fully
what ritual can be.

The Kaaba, the Muslim shrine at Mecca, the symbolic
connecting point of heaven and earth for the Islamic world,
is more fully comprehensible if we are familiar with the generic
theme of "world centers." Without a sense of that theme and
its prevalence, the Kaaba symbolism might be viewed merely
as an odd or unintelligible belief. By the same token, the
profound centering role of the Kaaba in the lives of Muslims
provides an extraordinary living illustration and amplification
of the world center motif.

The comparative process does not prejudge religious phenomena, as though they are there to be pinned and tagged
like helpless specimens that must be made to conform by all
means to our favorite taxonomies. Rather, religious expressions are facts—often living and articulate—that can continually instruct and illuminate our categories. In these ways,
comparative perspective is a larger educational and interpretive process than any simple, straightforward act of describing
or comparing different religions.

Plan of the Book

The following study is organized in two connected parts. The
first deals with the emergence of comparative concepts in the
modern period. It is intended to bring the reader to a place

where the second—which deals with large, comparative themes—will make sense.

To understand better the positioning, achievements, and features of the modern comparative study of religion—which first emerged in the nineteenth century and is now a part of many university liberal arts curricula—we examine first some traditional ways of interpreting religious diversity. Chapter 1 focuses on three major types of ideological comparison that were employed in the West before the rise of modern comparative religion and that are still represented in our culture: the Christian, rationalist, and universalist stances. The chapter also illustrates the point that all views of religious history are conditioned by historical and geographic horizons and that options for comparative perspective are therefore logically limited to the interpretive possibilities within those horizons. Well into the nineteenth century, for example, educated European Christians accepted a fixed classification of the entire religious world into four categories: Christianity, Judaism, Islam, and paganism—the latter defined by one author as "all those who have not the knowledge of the true God, but worship idols."[3] The acknowledgement of great, independent Asian religious traditions had simply not yet emerged, and the categories and prospects of impartial, global comparative work were essentially nonexistent.

Chapter 2 considers the emergence of the idea that religion is a subject matter in its own right. This "science of religion" movement—as it was called in Europe—was to go through several phases. But it can be roughly characterized by these indices: dispassionate objectivity with regard to religious data and comparison, including respect for accurate, primary source information; an affirmation that the subject matter of religion requires both historical and comparative (or systematic) analysis; and an affirmation that religion is a distinctive type of human activity. This approach introduced a new goal for comparative work: *understanding*.

The second part of the book is an examination of major, common forms and concepts that emerge from and in turn inform the understanding of religious life. Chapter 3 forms a transition to this material by focusing on a concept that is also both a result of and foundational to the entire comparative study of religion: the notion of religious systems as "worlds." World is the comparative category par excellence. All religions inhabit worlds constructed by their own particular religious symbols. Indeed, what the world "is" has traditionally been defined by religious language, though now science has taken over the task for many. *World* here is a descriptive word for what a community or individual deems is the "reality" it inhabits, not a term for some single system objectively "out there" that we all somehow share. The guiding principle of comparative study must be that each religious community acts within the premises of its own universe, its own logic, its own answers to its own questions. The concept of multiple worlds also helps us overcome some of the distortions that occur when we look at others only in terms of beliefs or doctrines. For religions are not just cognitive, conceptual affairs, to be compared with our own ideas and theologies, but matrices of action, ways of *inhabiting* a world.

While there are many legitimate and useful ways of classifying the forms of religious life, the four that we focus on here directly relate to the idea of religious worlds. Religious "reality" is primarily constituted through (1) mythic language and prototypes, (2) ritual times, (3) the engaging of gods, and (4) the distinction between pure and profane behavior. These forms of religious life, the forms of the sacred, are at one and the same time the forms of world construction and world expression. Though they have a degree of universality, our analysis will not try to show that they all "say" the same thing, but will bring out how they get filled with very different *content* in very different religious systems. They are the great themes, complex and internally differentiated, on which so many variations have been played.

The themes taken as a group provide a certain rounded view of religious life. They offer different lenses to observe the several dimensions of any religious system. All too often, interpretive models reduce religion to a single aspect—such as belief, feeling, or behavior.

Traditional Western treatments of the nature of religion typically divide the subject matter into topics such as creation, God, man, and the immortality of the soul, reflecting a biblical frame of reference. But to do justice to the subject matter, we need categories of analysis that are genuinely cross-cultural. Comparative work needs to go beyond approaches that simply set out to show how others approximate our *own* religious categories. The question here is not what "they" have to say about "our" ideas, but rather, what categories must we use in order to hear what others say?

Each of these chapters (4–7) show the general nature and significance of the theme it addresses. This requires cutting through some stereotypes and providing conceptual clarification since terms such as *myth* and *gods* are overlaid with many conflicting and ethnocentric uses. Once the theme becomes pertinent, once its applicability is engaged, then the variations can be seen in a new way. When cats, cars, or computers become useful, timely, or significant to us, so do their varieties. We look at them in a new, interested way. When artists become important to us, we approach each of their various creations with a certain relish. The same sense of relish can occur in the exploration of religious themes and their variations.

The concept of mythic language, described in chapter 4, is extraordinarily important in the study of religion. Religion has its own language, which should not be confused with scientific language. Myth articulates the foundations of what is sacred. It is not just a folktale about imaginary events, but an account of the origin of all that is thought to be great, real, or holy in one's universe. In addition, myth serves as the matrix of religious practice, of lived religious time and space, providing authoritative, sacred prototypes for human behavior. Every world has its own past, its own foundations, its account of "what happened at the beginning," and this is conveyed—whether orally or in scriptures—in the language of mythic events and symbols.

A second great organizing medium through which religious worlds receive expression is ritual time. Ritual shapes the sacred through action just as myth does through image and representation. Chapter 5 examines ritual not as a mechanical, magical attempt to manipulate imaginary forces, but as the deliberate structuring of action and time in order to give focus and expression to what is considered sacred. Ritual reconnects its participants with the sacred through (1) calendrical observances that renew what is foundational to the religious system, and (2) special observances that deal with changes or crises in one's world. By governing these two kinds of time, ritual shows itself to be an effective if not primary means of organizing and sacralizing the totality of experience. Because ritual times showcase what is ultimately significant in one's world, they are highly revealing to the comparativist. Often more concretely and intimately than myth, ritual shows just what it is that participants base their lives on.

Chapter 6 focuses on the role gods play in the structure and dynamics of religious worlds. Gods are specialized forms of mythic language and behavior that are important enough as a class to deserve special attention. The term *gods* is used here as a thematic label to include any beings that humans engage in a religious manner: buddhas, ancestors, spirits, gurus, as well as what we in the West usually think of as gods. Such beings are the significant "other" forces that confront humans and that humans must relate to in order to inhabit a world successfully and religiously. The endless variations on the theme "god" reveal an enormous diversity not only in terms of the domains of gods but also in the ways that gods and humans interact.

Chapter 7 deals with the theme of boundaries, epitomized in the polarity of pure/impure. Every religious system observes distinctions between proper and improper behavior, acts that foster sacred order and acts that diminish it. There are holy and unholy ways to live, and each culture will have its own native categories for this. For many years Westerners made invidious distinctions between "higher" ethical religion that focused on inner, moral purity and "lower" ritualistic religion that supposedly focused on physical, outward purity. While acknowledging the important difference between outer and inner domains of purity, we shall not cast this distinction into the form of a hierarchical model. Rather we shall propose that every world has its own good reasons for drawing the boundaries it does, for defining and dealing with its own forms of profanity and pollution. Purity, then, is interpreted broadly as the structuring or "separating" element in any system of religious behavior, and not just as a particular Judeo-Christian ethical ideal concerning sinlessness. Purity often stands for congruity, order, consistency. It can be expressed in the spheres of social roles or internal desires. We shall see how some religious systems even define purity in terms of freedom, the area to be "purified" or enlightened being one's own consciousness.

It is a primary aim of this study to show how such concepts not only provide a framework of intelligibility for religious phenomena but also generate the comparative perspective. Religious systems constitute autonomous worlds, are grounded in myth, expressed in ritual, include some types of engagement with mythic beings, and must deal with impurity or profanity in some way. Each of these structures, in turn, has limitless variations in content across many cultures.

The final chapter suggests some of the consequences of the comparative enterprise, looks at ways of interpreting the plurality of religious systems, and considers ways of handling issues about the relativity of the sacred.

Some Premises

It should be useful to state certain key premises of the book at the outset.

The term *religion* is generally used to mean a system of language and practice that organizes the world in terms of what is deemed sacred. This is a working characterization rather than a substantive definition. It does not attempt to pronounce what religion is in terms of some timeless essence. It describes religion as a phenomenon within the history of language, behavior, and world construction, and thus as a specific subject matter that can be investigated. The first emphasis of the statement is that religion is something people *do*. This differs in focus from approaches that define religion strictly in terms of what people believe. There is no metaphysical agenda here that gets installed by assuming a particular transcendental referent to all religion, and there is no rationalist insinuation that religion is some kind of primitive way to explain nature prior to the age of science. Whatever else religion may be said to be, it is at least a form of human behavior and language, a way of living in the world, and can be studied as such.

What characterizes religious behavior is that it takes place with reference to things that are *sacred*. If the old defining referent of religion was "God" (and most Western dictionaries still define religion as the worship of a supreme being), the more modern, cross-cultural term is *the sacred*. As used here, the term assumes neither the reality nor unreality of what is considered sacred, but simply the fact that people do *take* certain beings, traditions, principles, or objects to be sacred and these serve in turn as the organizing points of reference for defining their world and lives. The sacred can therefore have any content, though to the adherent it is always something of extraordinary power and reality.

Religious systems are designed to shape the overall way one perceives and construes existence. They do not merely define some limited realm of behavior within the world. As the sociologist Robert Bellah once put it, religion is "a set of symbolic forms and acts that relate man to the ultimate conditions of his existence."[4]

If religion is a system based on the sacred, then religiousness means the adherence to what is sacred. This interpretation is consonant with the Roman usage of the term *religio* to mean ritual observance or sacred, binding obligation.[5] The present book is as much about religiousness as it is about the more abstract category "religion." We will interpret the latter in terms of the former.

Religious life is its own expression, not to be reduced to the expression of something else. It is one of the tasks of the study of religion to investigate what is "religious" about religion—that is, to discern not only what is sacred but how the sacred is engaged—and not to explain away the subject matter from the start as simply a product of nonreligious (e.g., social) forces. This same type of distinction informs interpretive work in the parallel areas of art, music, and literature. Certainly religion *can* be explained as a social product. So can art. But that neglects the inner nature and content of the worlds posited by art and religion.

The field of religion has been fragmented by contending theories. Most of these theories try to reduce religion to one or another referent or function. Thus the essence of religion has been identified with explanation of the unknown, belief

in God, the awesome feeling of the supernatural, the sanctity
of collective authority, or the projection of solace. But it is
just this monolithic form of theorizing that has become out-
dated. There are fewer and fewer reasons any longer to take
these interpretations as mutually exclusive or to think that
the whole of religion must be boiled down to one dimension.
We are now in an eclectic age not by default but by choice,
and we have become quite accustomed to the idea of religion
as aspectual or multidimensional. Religion can involve feeling
and mystical experience, but also political, institutional structure. It may be about nature and it may be about self. It is
expressed in symbols and ideas, but also in acts and rites; in
art, and also in philosophies.

Interpretations of religion always have cultural locations.
They speak from those places and times in conversation with
the conceptual needs of a community. They create discourse
that not only expresses but in some way tries to re-create those
communities. Theory is relative to the educational, situational
needs of the society, the audience, or the reader. So with the
present study. Whether for good or ill, our time is one of
cultural pluralism and conceptual relativity, and this forms the
current context—one might even say opportunity—for learning and for liberal arts education.

Whatever the ultimate implications of a polycentric religious universe may be, the purpose of these chapters is to
describe a balanced, dispassionate view of the pluralistic character of religious systems and to show the resonant interaction
of key religious themes with their variations. Individual readers
will construe the relativity of the sacred in their own different
ways, within their own various worlds.

Part One

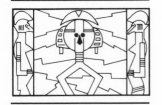

Religion and
Comparative Perspective

1

Some Traditional
Strategies of Comparison

INTERPRETATIONS of religious diversity have been conditioned by both geography and psychology. What is alien, contradictory, or inferior is always relative to one's territory and vistas. If one's horizon is only the Mediterranean, then the religions of that area will set the boundaries for comparison. We compare ourselves with what is visibly around us or with what—in our perception—went before us. China and India were simply not part of the worlds of the Bible and the Qur'an. But the widening of worldviews and the discovery of new religious continents provided completely new circumstances for the interpretation of others.

Until the early nineteenth century, Western culture still divided all religion into four kinds: Christianity, Judaism, Islam, and paganism. All that lay outside the biblical tradition, and its "great imposter, Mahometanism," was simply "idolatry." Today, in a much-expanded cultural universe, religion textbooks treat Judaism, Christianity, and Islam as the components of a single monotheistic tradition and compare that grouping with the religions of South and East Asia: Buddhism, Hinduism, Confucianism, and Taoism. The evolution of religious frontiers—beginning with travel reports, gaining momentum in the great ages of exploration, and finding consolidation in modern national blocks—kept re-creating the agenda for the comparative enterprise and led inevitably to the progressive dissolution of the concept of "pagan darkness."

Interpretation also has a certain existential or psychological motivation. The very existence of other worlds can be threatening. The history of "comparative" approaches to religion is part of the larger history of attitudes toward and projections on "the other." It is not always a pleasant history, but dealing with other worlds is an unavoidable part of human and religious experience. Other worlds and other gods do coexist with our own world and our own gods, and they are threatening precisely because they have a different set of premises from ours and thus explicitly or implicitly call into question the absoluteness of our own assumptions and commitments.

Otherness is a challenge that has always been met through the self-defensive activity of interpretation. The typical response to otherness—or foreignness—is to defuse it through explaining it in some fashion. Interpretation obviates the chaos of stark, anomic diversity by describing others in a way that makes them fit the interpreter's own ideology. Rare and late coming was the motivation to see the sacred systems of others in their own terms, according to their own essential ways of perceiving the world. So the multiple religious traditions of the world have lain in inaccessible darkness not only because of geographic distance but because of this shield of cognitive, self-protective bias. Thus do we make our own world safely inhabitable.

The rise of modern comparative religion is best understood against the backdrop of three traditional strategies of interpreting religious diversity. These approaches are ideological and are motivated by other than scientific purposes. They may be contrasted with the quite different, less political attitude present in the modern comparative study of religion.

The three most pervasive comparative stances found in the West may be labeled (1) Christian theology, (2) rationalism, and (3) universalism. Defenders of biblical religion have been necessarily concerned with the exact relationship, negative or positive, between what they take as their own unique revelation and the claims of other religions. Rationalists, the opposers of supernaturalism, used comparative material to undercut the supernatural, absolutist claims of biblical or other "revealed" religion and to reclassify religious history in terms that featured the emergence of an age of reason out of an age of primitive and religious superstition. Universalists are those who, from antiquity, have stressed the essential unity of all religion, interpreting all traditions to represent so many valid but varying versions of common spiritual truths. In the following sections we will consider samples of each of these three types of interpretation, without attempting a history of them.

Christian Comparisons

Biblical religion was based on the idea of a sequence of special divine revelations. It emerged in environments of religious competition, so that defensive self-positioning in relation to other religions became second nature. At the core of Christian doctrine is the affirmation of the definitive revelation of salvation in Christ, but even at the earliest periods of biblical faith there is the commandment to discriminate between false idols and the one true God: "You shall have no other gods before Me."

In the course of its history, Christianity has accounted for other religions in five different ways—namely, as (1) creations of evil forces, (2) explainable through historical diffusion from an original monotheism, (3) containing symbolic Christian truths, (4) demonstrably inferior in their practices and beliefs, and (5) expressing the innate, independent spiritual capacity of all humans to come to some understanding of the divine.

1. There were two variants on the "evil origins" explanation. The first was to interpret nonbiblical religion as demonstrative of humanity's fallen nature. Heathens were those persons and nations in a state of unredeemed darkness outside the penumbra of God's revelation. It was natural, therefore, that their beliefs and practices, visibly "abhorrent, cruel and absurd," would express the degenerate character of the adherents themselves. People without the true God will resort to their own self-serving, sinful nature, practice indulgent abominations of orgy and sacrifice, and believe in extravagant,

self-deceiving lies. They will create gods that satisfy their own lusts. All of this reflects the disgrace of human nature apart from true revelation. The 1796 edition of the *Encyclopaedia Britannica* still included the straight-faced information that "the festivals of the heathens were chiefly devoted to debauchery and idleness."[1]

Another version of evil origins was that other religions were specifically directed by demons or by Satan, the "Prince of this World." Pagan systems were in reality the mocking, conceited, and confusion-making work of the Devil and other fallen spirits. Pagan gods were demons, requiring in an aping way the same worship and devotion that should be rendered the true God. Many Christians were convinced that human sacrifices—in honor of these perverse deities—were offered up in most heathen countries around the globe. The very idea of pagan ritual conjured up licentious orgies and the image of parents burning their own children alive to satisfy the likes of Baal and Moloch. Moreover, the demons were incapable of novelty and could only imitate or corrupt the truth. Sixteenth-century Spanish missionaries declared the mockery of Satan when they encountered the iconographic Mayan crosses of Yucatan that had antedated the arrival of Christianity. "So what?" the crosses and Satan seemed to say. "We already knew what you are trying to bring us." Nor did the adversary confine his work to faraway primitives. Protestants were convinced that Satan was at work in the abominations of Catholicism. Martin Luther assailed both "the Pope and the Turk" as representatives of the devil. A Protestant book in 1826 titled *A Comparative View of Christianity* wrote of Islam and the "Popery" of Roman Catholicism: "Thus, Antichrist, in the right sense of the term, implying an opposition to all that can be called pure and vital religion, seems, from this period [seventh century] to have placed one of his feet on the Eastern and the other on the Western extent of Christendom."[2]

2. A second way of dealing with nonbiblical religions was through theories of historical diffusion. These could show that everything truly religious in religious history was in fact historically derived from the original monotheism of the biblical patriarchs, whereas everything false in other religions was a

degeneration from that once pure source. It was an approach that enabled Christians to acknowledge that there were admirable religious beliefs outside the fold while at the same time taking credit for them and thus depotentiating their effect as outside competition. It also provided a unified view of history, showing all humanity to be on a single continuum from a common starting point. There were several variants on this "historical" approach.

The first was that pagan religions could be explained as degenerations from a pure origin. For centuries the first eleven chapters of Genesis supplied the assumed historical backdrop for explaining the diffusion of different nations and religions, all of which were necessarily traced to the survivors of the Flood—that is, Noah and his three sons, Ham, Shem, and Japheth. Other religions, then, became the distorted, idolatrous versions of the original monotheism of Noah. Given this literal reading of biblical history, Christian "comparative religion" worked itself out with considerable ingenuity. It produced any number of theories explaining exactly how nations fell from an original lofty monotheism into a lower state— such as through the priestly manipulation of the masses, or through the contraction of perception from realities to mere symbols. Egyptian and Phoenician religion, for example, could be shown to stem from descendants of Noah's son Ham. These nations, "the first Nurseries of Idolatry," gradually "forgot" the one, true, transcendent God and began worshipping His powers and symbols in the sky, such as the sun and stars. In time their deviant religious veneration shifted to the deification of powerful objects on earth, such as animals, trees and plants, stones, and other parts of nature. Idolatry then spread to Chaldea, Mesopotamia, Asia Minor, and Greece, as the various heathen nations successively fell into error and folly.

If the idea of degeneration was one point of emphasis, the idea of outright plagiarism was another. Thus, Hesiod's mythic reference to a primal chaotic darkness was "stolen" from Genesis 1; and even pagan temple designs, it was charged, had been simply copied from the blueprint given to Moses on Sinai. Some writers interpreted the whole of the *Iliad* as "a pagan reworking of Joshua's assault against Jericho," and saw the adventures of Odysseus "as a transformed account of the wanderings of the patriarchs from the destruction of Sodom to Moses."[3]

In this diffusionist way, the many parallels and similar patterns perceived in religious history could be explained to Christian satisfaction. Works such as George Faber's *Origin of Pagan Idolatry Ascertained from Historical Testimony and Circumstantial Evidence* (1816)[4] traced virtually all symbols—whether religious or the literary imagery of epic and romance—back to the prototypical world of Noah: father gods were latter-day reflections of the patriarch himself; mother or earth goddesses were continuations of the symbolism of the ark (the original great mother, the earth); trinities such as the Hindu creator/preserver/destroyer recalled the three sons of Noah; and myths about the many cyclic renewals of the world were traced back to the cataclysm of the Flood. Faber labored to show how various symbolisms—such as the death of the great father, the union of the great father and the great mother, the rebirth of the great father—constituted distinct sets of images. Thus, the goddess of pagan mythology, however "multiplied according to the genius of polytheism," is ultimately one type of being, whether found in the Egyptian Isis or the Hindu Devi. All goddesses represent variations on the archetypal symbolism of sustenance, the nurturing earth and waters, the changing moon, the concept of enclosure (referring back to the ark), or the rule over animal life. Legends such as those referring to infant heroes being exposed in floating cases (again, arks) were systematically accounted for. Faber's work, in spite of its underlying derogatory distinction between pagan and "true" religion, amounted to a sustained investigation of the way imaginative literature repeats mythic archetypes.[5]

Still another variant of such "historical" explanation was euhemerism. This theory was first set forth in the third century B.C. by the Greek historian Euhemerus, who contended that the gods were really idealizations of great historical figures. He claimed, for example, that the god Zeus was originally an actual king of Crete. We can see now how the church fathers could gladly turn such a theory to their own service: all pagan gods could be understood as mythicized historical figures and thereby exposed as not being real gods at all. Non-Christian deities were only former pagan heroes and kings, or perhaps distant memories of biblical patriarchs. This theory had extraordinary influence and most Christian interpreters adopted some of its aspects. In the early Christian era it was used polemically, and in later centuries as a way of reconstructing global history.

Sometimes "etymologies" helped enhance the argument for historical derivations. Similarities in sounds of words gave grounds for tracing all religion back to its original source. The Egyptian god Ammon, for example, was clearly Noah's son, Ham. The Hindu Brahma must have originally been Abraham, and that the brahmans were descended from Abraham was "well known."[6] The god Serapis could be shown to have really been none other than the Hebrew forefather Joseph, on the grounds that Serapis equals *Sarras pais* ("Sarah's child"), and Sarah was Joseph's great-grandmother. And Atlas, of Greek mythology, was traceable to the biblical figure Lot, by demonstrating that the latter had become Lota in Phoenician, Otla by corruption, and finally Atlas.[7]

Finally, historical derivation was explained also through hypotheses about travel and contact. The presence of ideas resembling biblical religion among New World Indians could be accounted for through the supposition that there had been prior exposure to these ideas through travelers or missionaries. Much was written about the wanderings of the ten lost tribes of Israel and the travels of the apostles of Christ, showing how monotheistic ideas had been spread far and wide, only to be discovered in degenerate form hundreds of years later. In his *Customs of the American Indians Compared with the Customs of Primitive Times* (1724), the cautious Father Lafitau concluded that, although the theory that St. Thomas reached the New World must be considered conjectural, "it can be proven indeed, that, at the time when the Portuguese began to sail towards India, some vessel, carried towards Cape Verda by the rapidity of tempests which were frequent, may have been shipwrecked in Brazil and that some holy monk who may have survived the shipwreck, may have sown some seeds of the gospel in those countries."[8]

3. A third mode of Christian comparison involved seeing other religions as allegories of Christian truths. The Greeks

had already shown the possibilities of the allegorical interpretation of myths, but the precedent of Old Testament religion
also taught Christians how other faiths can "point to" the
truths of Christianity. All events in the Hebrew scriptures
were automatically assumed to "prefigure" the revelation of
Christ. The sacrifice of Isaac, for example, was seen as a "type"
of the sacrifice of Christ. Indeed, every ancient Hebraic sacrifice and oblation "shadowed forth" the death and passion of
the Messiah.

Similarly, the symbolic interpretation of nonbiblical religious symbols showed how Christian truths are concealed in
all traditions of the world. In 1648, Alexander Ross produced
an encyclopedia of heathen gods and heroes—listed serially
and comprehensively from A to Z—showing how every mythological figure contained some Christian lesson. "Achilles," he
writes, "was all dipt in the Stigian lake, except his feet; in
which onely he was vulnerable and mortal. Except we be all
washed in the Water of Baptism, we cannot be immortal."[9]
Apollo represents

> God himself, . . . for as they painted Apollo with his Harp,
> and the three Graces in one hand, with a Shield and two
> Arrows in the other; so by this perhaps, they meant that
> God was not only a punisher of wickedness, but a rewarder
> of goodness; as he had two arrows, so he hath many pun-
> ishments: But yet he hath the comfortable harp of his mercy
> to sweeten them in the other hand; and having but two
> arrows, hath three graces, to shew that he hath more mer-
> cies then punishments.[10]

In this fashion, attempts to reconcile Christianity and classical
mythology abounded. The different deities could be seen as
representing the various attributes of the one God. Athena
was God's wisdom. Themis was God's justice.

4. A fourth approach used by Christians was the attempt
to present an actual, objective demonstration of the superiority
of Christianity by producing comparative evidence about the
inferior nature of other religions. In this way, the religious
expressions of competitors get turned against themselves to
expose their own insufficiencies. A seventeenth-century Christian theologian wrote,

As the lustre of an Oriental Diamond is more clearly perceived, when compared with counterfeit Stones; so Christianity appears in its greatest Glory and Splendor, when
compared with the obscurity of Paganism: the Deformity of
the one, serving but as a foyl to the Beauty of the other.
Nor doth the Divinity of our Scriptures ever better appear,
than when compared with the Follies of the *Talmud*, and
Alcharon [the Qur'an], or the Constitutions of the Heathen
Law-givers.[11]

Different eras faced different competition. Church fathers
such as Origen and Ambrose had to argue against the credi-
bility of the leading Greco-Roman religions of the day. The
rise and success of Islam generated many Christian works demonstrating the false nature of this "imposter" religion. It was
argued, for example, that Islam could not be shown to fulfill
any biblical prophecies, that the alleged miracles attending its
rise could not be confirmed, and that the secrecy of Muhammad's revelations sharply contrasted with the public miracles
and voices attending Jesus' mission.[12] Because Muhammad
himself apparently had become the leading world rival of Jesus,
evidence was collected for the purpose of character assassi-
nation. To monogamist Christians, for example, Muhammad
with his several wives and concubines appeared "insatiably
lustful." He was pictured as a "crafty" man who had "feigned"
divine revelation in order to get personal power. In what was
perhaps the most popular textbook on world religions in the
seventeenth century, we find this example of how "Christianity exceeds Mahometanism as Jesus exceeds Mahomet":

The one being conceived of the holy Ghost, and born of
a Virgin; the other being conceived and born after the
manner of other men; the one being without sin, the other
a thief and robber; the one teaching love, peace and pa-
tience; the other hatred, war and revenge; the one curbing
men's lust by monogamy; the other letting loose the reins
to uncleanness by Polygamy; the one planting Religion in
the soul, the other in outward Ceremonies of the body: the
one permitting the moderate use of all God's creatures, the
other prohibiting wine, and swines flesh; the one com-
manding all men to search the Scriptures, the other prohibiting the vulgar to read the Alcoran, or to translate it

into other tongues out of the Arabick; the one working by
miracles; the other only by cheating tricks.[13]

The passage continues at length in making this sharp contrast
of positive and negative, light and dark.

Accounts of living "savage" tribes added even more exotic
and scandalous material for documenting the comparative
agenda. Christian interpreters described native practices and
beliefs in a way that made them appear manifestly perverse
and absurd, and by making other religions seem patently self-
condemning, this demonstrated the obvious supremacy of
Christianity all the more dramatically.

But arguing for the comparative superiority of Christianity
was carried on in ways both coarse and refined. By the nine-
teeth century it had become clear to many that the religious
systems of Asia were indeed impressive in their spiritual disciplines, and that the "civilized" religions of China and India
posed a more far-reaching religious challenge to Christians
than had the religions of antiquity, the primitives, or even
the kindred Jewish and Muslim monotheisms. James Freeman
Clarke's widely read *Ten Great Religions: An Essay in Comparative Theology,* first appearing in 1871, took up this challenge, and demonstrated a more scholarly, controlled form of
theological comparison.[14] For Clarke, the contrast between
Christianity and other religions was not that between the
sublime and the ridiculous, but between the completely true
and the partially true, between the perfect and the imperfect.
With new knowledge of Asian religions and scriptures, wrote
Clarke, Christianity would no longer have to rely on mere
assertion or scriptural miracles to show its supremacy, for now
it could do so by direct, fair comparison of itself with others.
He stressed that Christians could not go back to an ignorant,
blanket disparagement of others, but must understand the
strengths of other religions—as being "schoolmasters for
Christ"—as well as their weaknesses. He construed "comparative theology" as a kind of science of missions. For Clarke,
comparison demonstrated that Christianity embodies greater
transethnic universality and more complete spiritual balance
than other religions. Thus Hinduism has a full sense of the
reality of the spirit, but it is "defective" in its appreciation of

matter and the created world. Buddhism appreciates man's nobility, but it misses the dimension of divinity in the world. Confucianism understands religious harmony, but it lacks historical dynamism and vision. And so on. Christianity for its part is complete and universal, free of the specific faults and one-sidedness of other faiths, recognizing both the transcendental and incarnational aspects of God, both the human and divine sides of truth, both the eternal and historical dimensions of life. It therefore represents the consummate fullness of all religion.

5. Not all Christian comparison has been belittling. Some of the earliest theologians were drawn to a doctrine that focused on the positive relation of their faith to others. The doctrine of the *Logos* or immanent Word of God, referred to in the Bible,[15] conveyed the idea that the divine is present in the whole of creation and that every human innately bears the image of God. Because of this natural endowment, and the capacity to reason, all people can come to some natural truths about the divine being. The idea was believed to be clearly confirmed and illustrated in the virtuous lives and elevated religious concepts of the great Greek and Roman moral philosophers who had had no knowledge of Christianity. Later, in the seventeenth and eighteenth centuries, this concept gave support to the distinction between "natural religion" and "revealed religion"; the former represents the religious sentiments common to all of mankind, and the latter refers to the specially revealed truths of the Bible. A modern, ecumenical statement of this idea was expressed in a document of the Second Vatican Council (1963–1965), which not only urged Catholics to appreciate the presence of "the holy" in other traditions, but also established a permanent commission to study the matter and explore it through dialogue.[16] Current analysis about the relation of Christianity to other faiths abounds.[17]

In summary, Christians have viewed other religions with different degrees of suspicion and appreciation, and with varying kinds of interpretive strategy. But they have always done so in terms of a fixed, unifying world commitment of their own and always in relation to the current horizon of perceived "competition."

Rationalism: Turning the Tables

Comparative theories of religion not only became ways for defending faith, but also for undermining it. Rationalism is a general label for those interpretations that, regarding reason as man's highest faculty and achievement, oppose any super-natural explanations of religious history and see the age of religion as giving way to an age of science. Such secular theo-rizing appeared with certain Greek and Roman philosophers who believed that all gods and myths could be explained as projections of the human mind. It is well represented in the modern age of Enlightenment, an age which continues to challenge Christian claims.

One stage in the development of the rationalist approach was the emergence of Deism in seventeenth- and eighteenth-century England and France. Deism formed a kind of halfway house between Christianity and liberal modernity. On the one hand, Deists discredited supernaturalist interpretations of his-tory; but on the other hand, they maintained that belief in a supreme architect of the universe and the ideal of love were the highest forms of religion humans could achieve. For our purposes, it is notable that Deism was scathing in the way it applied to Christianity itself many of the arguments that had been made previously against paganism. Accepting the idea that much of mankind was in religious error, it added most of the history of Christianity to the list, seeing little discontinuity between Judeo-Christian and primitive religion. Voltaire (1694–1778), pointing to the "ridiculous" behavior of many Christians, asked, "How dare they make fun of Laplanders, Samoyedes, and Negroes!"[18] In *The Natural History of Religion*, David Hume (1711–1776) wrote, "The human sacrifices of the Carthaginians, Mexicans, and many barbarous nations, scarce exceed the inquisition and persecutions of Rome and Madrid."[19] Hume imagined a Catholic divine and an Egyptian priest in dialogue:

> How can you worship leeks and onions [asks the Catholic]?
> If we worship them, replies [the Egyptian], at least we do
> not, at the same time, eat them. But what strange objects
> of adoration are cats and monkeys? says the learned doctor.
> They are at least as good as the relics or rotten bones of

martyrs, answers his no less learned antagonist. Are you not mad, insists the Catholic, to cut one another's throat about the preference of a cabbage or a cucumber. Yes, says the pagan: I allow it, if you will confess, that all those are still madder, who fight about the preference among volumes of sophistry, ten thousand of which are not equal in value to one cabbage or cucumber.[20]

For European rationalists, religious history could now be written free of Christian authority. The pursuit of "natural" histories of religion was often accompanied with revolutionary indignation and liberative zeal.

The comparative method played a new role in the rationalist's approach. It was used as a weapon. It was used to turn the tables on the Christian apologists. Primitive and Christian phenomena could now be examined as examples of the same errors, not as separate domains. Notice how this figures into Sir James G. Frazer's preface to the 1900 edition of *The Golden Bough*, an enormous work attempting, among other things, to show the primitive foundations and patterns of religious ideas:

> It is indeed a melancholy and in some respects thankless task to strike at the foundations of beliefs in which, as in a strong tower, the hopes and aspirations of humanity through long ages have sought a refuge from the storm and stress of life. Yet sooner or later it is inevitable that *the battery of the comparative method* should breach these venerable walls, mantled over with the ivy and mosses and wild flowers of a thousand tender and sacred associations. At present we are only dragging the guns into position: they have hardly yet begun to speak. The task of building up into fairer and more enduring forms the old structures so rudely shattered is reserved for other hands, perhaps for other and happier ages.[21] [Italics added]

Rationalists liked to show that whatever one religion, like Christianity, could boast of as its unique possession—like having a God-sent savior or a doctrine of salvation by divine grace—was also present in other religions. For example, the author of a book on comparative religion written in 1877 writes,

> Nothing can be said by a Christian, on behalf of the in-
> spiration of his Scriptures, which might not be said by the
> Buddhist, the Confucian, or the Mussulman on behalf of
> the inspiration of theirs. If his appear to him more beautiful,
> more perfect, more sublime, so do theirs to them; . . . So
> it is in reference to miracles. Christianity can point to no
> miracles tending to establish its truth, which may not be
> matched by others tending to establish the truth of rival
> creeds.[22]

Every religion, this writer continues, has the same appeal to
sacred "evidence" and authority for its exclusive truth, and
all nations have accounts of the absolute power of their divinities. The conclusion is:

> Under the touch of a comparative anatomy of creeds, all
> that was imposing and magnificent in the edifice of theology
> crumbles into dust. Systems of thought piled up with elab-
> orate care, philosophies evolved by centuries of toilsome
> preparation, fall into shapeless ruins at our feet. And all
> this by the simple process of putting them side by side.[23]

If the comparative process had been used by Christians to
defuse the authority of other religions, it was now used by the
rationalists to defuse Christian absolutism.

Hume, Frazer, and other spokesmen for the Enlightenment inverted the Christian idea that religious history had an
original period of pure monotheism from which things degen-
erated. They showed that all religion had primitive origins.
Idolatry here turns out to be the original religion of humanity.
The concept of evolution was used to show that biblical religion had its infancy and development in the cruder, archaic
phases of human mentality. The rationalists maintained that
religious history began with a reliance on magic, the worship
of the dead, the veneration of objects in nature, and polytheism. The central symbols of Christianity itself could be shown
to have prerational, "pagan" roots. Wrote the archrationalist
Freud, "Comparative research has been struck by the fatal
resemblance between religious ideas which we revere and the
mental products of primitive peoples and times."[24]

As Christians explained away paganism, so the rationalists
explained away all supernatural religion by showing that it

was traceable to the fears, wishes, and mistaken reasonings of prescientific humanity. Whereas Christian theories had differentiated true and false religion and had given their own faith a privileged place, rationalists recognized no such special compartments. Inevitably, comparison here came to have a subversive function.

In their attempt to counteract Christian claims, European rationalists could not avoid imposing their own ideological world on religious worlds and forcing their own unifying schemas on religious history. In every instance of rationalist theory, we find the need to trace religion to a single source, either within human nature or to some factor in social evolution. Rather than the original monotheism of Noah, religion was derived from "fetishism" (Charles de Brosses), from veneration of the forces and imagery of nature (Dupuis), from ancestor reverence (Spencer), from class conflict (Marx), from the sacredness of collective values (Durkheim), or from psychological immaturity (Freud). Most influential of all was Edward B. Tylor's theory of animism, set forth in his *Primitive Culture* (1871), showing how religion evolved from the belief in souls and spirits. By the early twentieth century, rationalist theories had reduced religion—regardless of the distinction between biblical and nonbiblical types—to every conceivable kind of social and individual need.

Universalism

The third Western framework for viewing the diversity and genealogy of religions is universalism. Universalism is an apt enough term for those views affirming that all religions contain common spiritual realities or at least have different paths to the same goal. Universalism stands against what it perceives to be parochialism. Behind the facades of local religious divergence it finds universal points of agreement. It finds all religions pointing to the same idea of a supreme—usually divine—reality. Universalism is a position that became highly developed in classical Stoicism and Neoplatonism, and was fostered by various forms of romanticism and transcendentalism. It has been a basic premise of many Asian traditions.

In the ancient world there was a well-known doctrine of "the equivalence of the gods." Thus the fifth century B.C. Greek historian Herodotus assumed that the neighboring Egyptian gods were simply that country's names for the Greek divinities that governed the world. Ammon was simply the Egyptian name for Zeus, Horus was really Apollo, Isis was Demeter, and Osiris was Dionysus. Julius Caesar referred to the main god of the Celts as Mercury, and Tacitus easily spotted his own Hercules and Mars among the Germans. The gods of others were not really foreign at all, but just different names for the same universal principles, or in some cases names for different attributes of the same divine being. The Neoplatonic tradition, distinguishing an eternal world of divine being—"the One"—from a changing world of relative and material truths—"the Many"—provided a metaphysical basis for universalist ideas and was revived as an influence during the Renaissance.

Deism was not only a source of rationalist ideas but also of certain forms of universalism. For, while one facet of the movement formed an attack on conventional religious claims, another stressed that there was an underlying, higher, universal "natural religion" common to all human societies. All forms of Deism would agree that there have been two levels of religious consciousness manifest in culture—that of the enlightened and wise and that of the ignorant masses. The first understand the higher notion of a supreme being; the latter traffic in superstitious, vulgar, or fanatical notions about miracles and magic. On religious matters, the masses will disagree, but the wise and truly saintly will agree. In the eighteenth century, Confucian writings—with their concepts about conformity to heavenly harmony—were often cited as an example of the enlightened level that "natural religious man" can reach in cultures far removed in space and time from Christianity. One of the many attempts to sift out the universal, enduring elements of religious belief from the "chaff" of arbitrary and culturally relative claims was that of "the father of Deism," Herbert of Cherbury (1582–1648). Herbert made a sustained case for the existence of five common religious truths present everywhere: the acknowledgement of the existence of God, the duty of worshipping Him, the idea that piety and virtue are the chief parts of divine worship, the value of repentance of sins, and the idea of punishment and reward both in this life and after death.

Where Christians saw biblical prototypes as the source of all that is pure and good in religious history, universalists often exalted other cultures and traditions as founts and standards of religious wisdom. Some found the "great time" in the days of the Greek gods, whereas others (the German romantics, especially) saw Egypt, China, or India as the source of profound, universal religious truths. Thus one school held that Moses learned his religious ideas from the mystical brotherhoods of Egypt, and another exuberant theory declared that the five books of Moses, along with the five Confucian classics, were simply derivations from the five Hindu Vedas.[25]

Asian religions have been a source of much of the universalist thinking of the twentieth-century West. For classic Hinduism, all life is a manifestation of the one divine being, Brahman, and the millions of gods are the many faces by which Brahman appears to finite consciousness. The nineteenth-century saint Sri Ramakrishna was a famous spokesman for Hindu universalism:

> "I have practised," said he, "all religions—Hinduism, Islam, Christianity—and I have also followed the paths of the different Hindu sects. I have found that it is the same God toward whom all are directing their steps, though along different paths . . . . Wherever I look, I see men quarrelling in the name of religion—Hindus, Mohammedans, Brahmos, Vaishnavas, and the rest. But they never reflect that He who is called Krishna is also called Shiva, and bears the name of the Primal Energy, Jesus, and Allah as well— the same Rama with a thousand names. A lake has several ghats. At one the Hindus take water in pitchers and call it 'jal'; at another the Mussalmans take water in leather bags and call it 'pani.' At a third the Christians call it 'water.' Can we imagine that it is not 'jal,' but only 'pani' or 'water'? How ridiculous! The substance is one under different names, and everyone is seeking the same substance; only climate, temperament and name create differences."[26]

This is why Hinduism has a way of absorbing other religions. Christian missionaries could not make much headway in a

land where Christ was readily accepted as just one more incarnation or *avatara* of the supreme universal god Vishnu. And
for their part, many Hindu missionaries in the West claim
that they are not so much trying to draw Westerners away
from the biblical religions as much as to help them find the
deeper, universal elements therein.

In the Far East, indigenous Chinese and Japanese gods
were commonly interpreted by Buddhists as "manifestations"
of cosmic buddhas and bodhisattvas. For example, Amaterasu,
the great Japanese sun goddess, was identified as an embodiment of the Buddha Maha-Vairocana. Buddhas were the "orig-
inals," where the *kami* (gods) of Shintoism were their
"appearances." Later Shintoists reversed this relationship.

Many Westerners have found a "perennial philosophy"—
as in the title of Aldous Huxley's book on the subject—embodied in mystical experience and writings around the globe.
Huxley stressed that the mystics of all religions express a common unity of vision because they have all alike experienced
the one reality "beyond name and form." Innumerable religious sects have maintained versions of the idea of a traditional
wisdom that underlies all historical religions and have emphasized the great difference between parochial, literal interpretations of religion, on the one hand, and mystical or
symbolic interpretations on the other.

In the twentieth century, Carl Gustav Jung (1875–1961)
developed a psychological approach to religion and mythology
that stressed the role of universal, collective archetypes embodied in every psyche. The myths and gods here represent
typical functions of the unconscious that get reenacted over
and over again in similar ways in individual lives. Everywhere
we find versions of the great mother, the hero, the tyrant
father—all representing structures of the relationship of the
ego and the unconscious. The archetypal self that is in all of
us is "The Hero with a Thousand Faces," as Joseph Campbell
puts it in the title of his widely read book.[27] The stages of the
journey of the human spirit follow the same patterns, with but
local variations, everywhere.

Biblical comparison. Rationalist comparison. Universalist
comparison. These three positions are still quite alive. They

still represent the common ways Westerners interpret religious diversity. Each stance has its evolving contexts of application. Each has its characteristic situational purposes and logic, its own comparative agendas, its own interpretive solutions. Biblical faith will always face the question of its relationship to other faiths. Rationalism and universalism in their different ways continue the attempt to overthrow or transcend the narrowness of traditional religious claims and dogma.

But these are only the typical approaches in the West. How much more complex it would be to try to summarize all the different approaches to religions as known to other cultures. Islam, for example, has its own complex history of interpreting other faiths. Yet the following hypothesis may be ventured. In the modern world, each culture is apt to have interpretations of religions that (1) represent the "hometown" faith (e.g., Christianity, Islam, Buddhism, or Judaism), (2) subvert the absoluteness of that faith, and (3) overcome the provincialness of that faith through some kind of universalism.

But this is still far from the whole story of comparative approaches.

This outline of traditional comparative styles prepares us to consider a fourth approach, one that is not aimed at using the history of religion to illustrate a predetermined ideology. The comparative study of religion—as we will refer to it in the following chapters—has an expressly noncontentious aim: *understanding*. It is not just one more theory alongside the other three, but differs from them in kind. The history of religions here is approached not as a field for metaphysical gerrymandering but as a subject matter in its own right.

2

Religion as a Subject Matter

A New Approach to Religion

The phrase "science of religion" sounds odd today. The two terms do not seem to belong together. But a century ago this rather presumptuous expression had become a banner announcing that religion, like history and society, was now a subject matter that could be investigated in an objective manner and not just left to the church, rationalist critics, and speculative philosophy. This new approach differs from the other three because it adopted the paradigms of impartial inquiry in place of any a priori schemas of metaphysical interpretation. We will outline the movement in broad terms, identifying—from retrospective vantage—the main conceptual trajectories that formed its modern position.[1]

Although adherents of this approach have tended to accept some of the ideological concerns of either the biblicist, rationalist, or universalist viewpoints, the aims of the movement per se represented an altogether different focus and purpose. For the first time religion became a field of genuine inquiry, something to be studied and understood, and not just a proving ground for self-defensive theorizing. Those Europeans who worked toward a science of religion were often liberal Christians by cultural inheritance, but they made attempts at objectivity by not confusing their own beliefs with their study of others. With figures such as F. Max Müller (1823–1900),[2] rightly honored as the father of the comparative religion movement, religion ceased to be a matter of speculative judgment and became a field of knowledge with demanding requirements for those who would honestly pursue it.

The distinguishing mark that separated "scientific" from other kinds of comparison was the emphasis on an objective understanding of the material itself. As biblicists opposed false religion, as rationalists opposed unenlightened beliefs, and as universalists opposed parochialism, so the "science" of religion—and how different and unusual was this incentive—opposed the priority of theory to investigation. As Müller pointed out, "Before the rise of geology it was easy to speculate on the origin of the earth."[3] Imperfectly at first, to be sure, this new discipline set out to replace the dogmatic theories that had ruled so long and to create its own equivalent of geology.

To pursue a science of religion meant taking a position that might well give offense to both the theological and rationalistic camps. Müller had critics from both. On the one hand were those who thought religion "too sacred a subject for scientific treatment"; on the other were those who put it "on a level with alchemy and astrology, a mere tissue of errors or hallucinations, far beneath the notice of a man of science."[4] Today the comparative study of religion still attempts to stake out a neutral ground.

This nontheological approach to religious diversity has had various names. Besides the "science of religion"—a term rarely used now in the English-speaking world—these include "the history and phenomenology of religion," "the history of religions," and "comparative religion."

Certainly the idea of "objective" collections of knowledge was present in some ways before the nineteenth century. Twenty-five hundred years ago Herodotus had gathered and classified religious facts from all societies known to him at the time. The sixteenth century produced an effusion of works on "customs and rites of all peoples," concomitant with the new encyclopedic tradition of bringing together the broadest range of materials about human cultures. Although most of these works indulged in the exotic aspects of the material—along the lines of the "curiosity cabinets" that housed wonders and artifacts from around the globe—occasionally we find individual works on religion prior to Max Müller's time that made efforts at impartiality. In a conspicuously rare attempt to present the phenomena in as fair a way as possible, an 1801 compilation describing "every known religious system in the world" begins:

> The reader will be pleased to observe, that the following rules have been carefully adhered to through the whole of this performance.
>
> 1st. To avoid giving the least preference of one denomination above another: omitting those passages in the authors cited, where they pass their judgment on the sentiments, of which they give an account: consequently the making use of any such appellations, as Heretics, Schismatics, Enthusiasts, Fanatics, etc. is carefully avoided.
>
> 2nd. To give a few of the arguments of the principle sects, from their own authors, where they could be obtained.
>
> 3d. To endeavour to give the sentiments of every sect in the general collective sense of that denomination.
>
> 4th. To give the whole as much as possible, in the words of the authors from which the compilation is made, and where that could not be done without too great prolixity, to take the utmost care not to misrepresent the ideas.[5]

But only in the late nineteenth century could religion become a field of knowledge per se. As the physical world had become an object of investigation rather than belief, so too the human, historical world had its explorers and mapmakers to discover, chart, and analyze its contents. Religion has always been interpreted. Yet the horizons of these interpretations were seriously confined. When Columbus discovered America, he thought he had found Asia and the earthly paradise. He conceived of everything he found as a version of the worldview or mythology he brought with him. Likewise, when the first Neanderthal skeleton was found in 1856, there was no accurate historical framework for interpreting what it really was. Because of the bowed legs, some thought it was a Cossack. Others were sure it was a bear. Encounters with the religions of others evoked analogous responses and verdicts.

The so-called science of religion was part of a wider, burgeoning enthusiasm about comparative method. Müller and others held that comparative religion is to any one religion as comparative philology is to the study of any particular language and as comparative anatomy is to any special anatomy. As the life sciences made progress through application of this method, so too would religious inquiry. Müller liked to apply to religion what Goethe said of language: "he who knows one . . . knows none."[6]

But the movement could not have taken place without the catalytic effect of the availability of accurate, primary-source knowledge about Asian religions. It was this, above all, that created the possibility of a truly global, comparative perspective. The older, parochial Western view of religious history as a contest of biblical and pagan traditions was becoming obsolete. It is pertinent that Müller himself was a scholar and translator of oriental texts and the editor of the great *Sacred Books of the East* translation series. The "other half" of the literate, religious world could now represent itself through its own texts. The East could state its own religious positions in its own religious terms, and this gradually eroded the provincial idea that Western monotheism is the only paradigm of human religiousness. Here were Buddhist and East Asian traditions that functioned well without the notion of deity, and here were religiously "sophisticated" scriptures such as the Tao Te Ching, the Upanishads, and the Bhagavad Gita, which appeared to rival Western Bibles in spiritual scope and depth. All of this showed the inadequacy of a merely Western-style, in-house knowledge of "religion." So it was not travelers' tales of gruesome and licentious savage practices but scholarly translations of oriental scriptures and respectable university chairs in comparative studies that now launched the possibility of broad civilizational comparisons and provided an historical foil for viewing the biblical monotheisms in wider context.

Contributing to this widening lens were the reports of field anthropologists that depicted "primitive" peoples not as idolaters or oddities but as distinctive communities with their own worldviews—that is, as different configurations of what it means to be a human culture inhabiting an environment. Each such society had its own self-defining central values and ritual system. Learning the actual language of that world was the prerequisite for an outsider who wished to understand it on its own terms. Thus the breakdown of European ethnocentrism, the widespread relativizing of biblical beliefs, and the acceptance of culture as something plural, all proceeded at a steady pace. Anthropologists and historians opened up the worlds of thousands of societies in time and space, making the study of "religion" all the richer and unlimited in comparative material and vistas.

The study of religion in the last hundred years has unfolded in different phases. Most useful, though, for our purposes, is to gain a synoptic view of the key conceptual ingredients of the field as a total legacy. We focus therefore on four affirmations that have become cornerstones of the modern comparative approach: (1) respect for all religious facts as "phenomena" rather than as items that are intrinsically true or false; (2) the need to synthesize these facts through the analysis of patterns; (3) the need to understand religious expressions in terms of their contexts; and (4) underlying the whole enterprise, the need to identify what it is about religious facts that makes them religious.

Religion as Subject Matter

The bedrock, first principle of this new comparative study of religion was the regard for all religious expressions as phenomena, without privileged position. This meant that religious practices and representations were not viewed as mere exotica, fictions, or samples of eternal truths; rather they were viewed as facts to be noted and understood. The enthusiasm that first led Müller in 1867 to speak of the possibility of a science of religion came from his awareness that a windfall of hitherto unknown continents of facts had become available. He had seen the new horizons, the new religious geography, and it was with the oriental texts in hand that he could challenge the merely speculative interpretations of world religions advanced by philosophers and establish firmly the distinction between amateur opinion and professional expertise regarding the history and comparison of religions. J. G. Frazer also embodied some of the new, scientific attitude, likening the comparative task of his age to that of "pioneers hewing lanes and clearings in the forest where others will hereafter sow and reap."[7] The author of a book titled *The Evolution of Religion* (1894) reminded readers, "The work of science is to find law, order and reason in what seems at first accidental, capricious and meaningless, and the arduousness of that work grows with the complexity and intricacy of the phenomena to be explained."[8]

The method of dealing with religious material will differ from that of the laboratory sciences because the facts are of a different order than those of the physical world. Like the other expressions of the humanities, they are facts that invite understanding more than experimentation. William James's classic, *The Varieties of Religious Experience* (1901–2), presented a careful documentation of firsthand accounts of religious experiences, establishing that here were indeed facts of a definite and irreducible kind, deserving the same impartial analysis as anything a physical scientist could observe. His attentiveness to both the varieties and nuances of these materials and his fastidious attempts to understand different types of religious experience such as conversion and asceticism made his book a model of objectivity and showed for the first time that mystical experience was itself not just something to be taken as true or illusory but constituted a set of data for research and comparison.

The idea of bracketing out one's biases in order to allow religious expressions to present themselves in their own terms was given special emphasis by the continental "phenomenology of religion" movement, especially as epitomized by the Dutchman Gerardus van der Leeuw (1890–1950).[9] Phenomenological knowing requires setting aside one's own natural but intervening and judging attitudes in order to get at the content of other human experience. Although some religion scholars came to think of neutral, "value-free" analysis as an end in itself, others emphasize neutrality not so much to stress scientific purity but to underscore open-mindedness as a way of access to the actual content—the point, or meaning—of the subject matter. Either way, the main concern is to show that religious structures do exist in human experience and how they exist, and not be obstructed at the outset with the issue of whether those structures have a referent in some outside reality or not. So the phenomenological study of religion leaves aside the question of metaphysical interpretation, while looking carefully at what the "reality" *means* to the participant—for this is the real phenomenon.

Phenomenologists of religion took their subject matter to be the experience of the sacred or holy. The major twentieth-century figure in the discipline, Mircea Eliade (1907–1986),[10] introduced the term *hierophanies* (literally, "manifestations of the sacred") to refer to these situations. For what Christians once called idolatry and what rationalists still call erroneous belief are actually someone's experience of the sacred through a particular object or symbol. Thus animals, stones, trees, and consecrated bundles of feathers are not worshipped in themselves but insofar as they represent the sacred. Such occurrences have a kind of absoluteness, whether embodied in humble, local objects or in mystical visions of the identity of the whole cosmos with God. Whether hierophanies take place in meditative states or in public ceremonies, each paradoxically brings together the sacred and the world, the supernatural and the natural, into a single religious fact, and the history of religions is the history of such phenomena.

Patterns and Typologies: Synthesizing the Facts

Along with the basic idea of religion as a "subject matter" came the corollary that this material has recurring structures and forms that can be accurately classified and analyzed. There had always been classifications, but classification itself is not necessarily synonymous with objectivity or impartiality. That all nonbiblical gods are demons, or historical heroes, is certainly a form of classification, as is the idea that each Greek god "represents" a certain virtue or vice. The untutored person on the street has his or her own "classification" of local religious pheonomena. But synthesizing factual material in the even-handed spirit of genuine inquiry was a new ideal.

Comparative analysis in the study of religion was to develop over several decades. The initial synthesizing activity that went under the name of the new science had to be general classification. One first had to have an accurate map and an accurate genealogy. Prior to the nineteenth century, when scriptures were still the operating model for human history (and most of the "outside" world was still in the shadows), there could be no basis for an accurate historical perspective and grouping of religions. Clearly, one of the first organizational tasks was to sort out how the different religions actually relate to each other historically and typologically. New family trees were needed to replace the old histories of paganism. One early attempt followed the model of comparative philology. Müller, reminding his audiences that it was no longer defensible to trace all languages back to Hebrew, and pointing to the newly understood genealogy of the Indo-European languages, tried to distinguish groupings of religions that paralleled real language traditions.

Many comparativists adopted evolutionary schemas that placed successive kinds of religions on a scale of simple to advanced or material to spiritual. And many believed with Edward Tylor that religion could be shown to begin with simple animism, the belief that things have spirit, proceed through polytheism, and arrive at monotheism. By the turn of the century it was clear that formulas such as this imposed monotheistic criteria onto history, and in time the "from lower to higher" schemas were abandoned.

But another form of comparative work was emerging. At the same time that religious history was being reclassified, scholars began to work out taxonomies or "phenomenologies" of religion: classifications of the common structures of religious life. Modern morphologies of religion trace themselves directly back to an encyclopedic work by P. D. Chantepie de la Saussaye published in 1887 and translated as the *Manual of the Science of Religion*.[11] In this influential text, a large section on the various categories of religious life was included alongside the sections describing each individual religion. The first section Chantepie called "phenomenological," and it grouped together and described "classes" of religious "phenomena." These included typical objects of veneration, such as stones, trees, animals, sky, earth, sun, moon, fire, ancestors, saints, heroes, and gods, as well as practices, such as divination, sacrifice, prayer, sacred dance and music, processions, rites of purification, and sacred times and places. Also included was cross-cultural documentation of categories such as priests (and other specialists), scriptures, types of religious communities, myths, and theologies. Chantepie illustrated each category with examples from different cultures, and summarized the research that had been done on that class of phenomena. This began what may be called the anatomical approach to religion, opening up possibilities of thematic study that went beyond just the description of different historical traditions. Emerging here was the idea that forms of religious practice and sym-bolization were as appropriate an object of study as individual "religions."

These new attitudes toward patterns replaced earlier lists of exotica. What Linnaeus had done for the botanical world was now being done for religion. The world of the sacred had to be mapped and its species, its "classes of phenomena," named and typed.

Yet typological study was not limited to doing inventories. It was also used to help understand history. An influential application of the morphological perspective to biblical ma-terials was Robertson Smith's controversial *Religion of the Sem-ites* (1889).[12] In 1880, Smith had been suspended from his professorship at the University of Aberdeen for the dangerous act of incorporating biblical religion into the historical/com-parative view. His study of ancient biblical religion within the context of ritual patterns in the Near Eastern environment showed the applicability of comparative categories such as holiness, taboo, sacred places, and sacred stones and trees in understanding early Hebrew religion.

Also influential for showing the usefulness of comparative method was Frazer's *Golden Bough* (first ed., 1890). Frazer began by citing an obscure Roman ritual that involved the rules of succession to the priesthood of Diana in a grove outside Rome. The custom concerned the need for the new priest to kill the old priest before taking his place and to do so in connection with the plucking of a golden bough. The entire, voluminous *Golden Bough* (coming to eleven volumes in the third edition) was, by Frazer's stated purpose, an attempt to throw light on this one ritual by marshaling cross-cultural materials that addressed similar themes. The book's sections dealt at length with sacred kingship, ritual death, and the ritual renewal of life through plant and other fertility symbols. Even though his methods of gathering material do not hold up to modern standards, Frazer supplied the apparently incomprehensible ancient Roman rite with a comparative context and thus a certain intelligibility.

Twentieth-century scholars developed new uses of comparative perspective that went well beyond these earlier concerns for parallels and classification. The need to group classes of things was succeeded by the need to understand the religious meaning of the patterns themselves. This was exemplified in the works of van der Leeuw and Eliade, the two most influential comparativists of the modern period. Through the use of cross-cultural material, each tried to demonstrate the religious character and function of the forms of religious life. What were just classes of phenomena for their predecessors, such as types of ritual and symbol, became understood here as vehicles or modalities of the experience of the sacred. Forms of religious life, such as sacrifice and cosmogonies, were shown to be intrinsically connected with the context of the experience of the sacred (or holy), a context inviting special inquiry and understanding.

Van der Leeuw emphasized the method and goal of understanding. In his enormous work *Religion in Essence and Manifestation* (1933) he did not hesitate to cite poetry, parts of private letters, or principles of gestalt psychology in order to express or amplify his understanding of the religious significance of some 106 religious forms. So this was not just the organizational program of placing similar phenomena together into different boxes (as with Chantepie), but a searching analysis of the religious value or function of each form.

Eliade emphasized that patterns such as cosmogonic myths, annual renewal rites, initiation rites, and symbolisms of "the center," the sky, and the earth, form systems of their own. These systems are discovered through seeing the history of values placed on them. Knowing these histories in turn supplies a context for appreciating any one particular symbol.

The studies of patterns and history are thus complementary. The history of any symbol or ritual will show both continuity and innovation—that is, the innumerable ways societies create versions of common themes.

The symbolism of the center or axis of the world is an example. Eliade wrote a great deal about structures and objects that were taken to represent the center of the world. He found that all over the world there was a belief that one's own ritual or ceremonial center was the "navel of the universe," connecting heaven and earth, humans and gods, affording an opening or passage to the divine. The center could be a mountain, a temple, or a shrine. It could be portable or fixed. Around the center the world becomes habitable, oriented. Most religious systems will have their own versions of such an axis. When we find "navel of the world" or "center of the world" language, then, we are witness to an archetype at work, not a mistake in logic. The existence of many world centers leads us to appreciate the general motivation for creating an axis in space, and it helps us understand any particular version of such space as an embodiment of the ongoing, thematic, human need for cosmic orientation. The Muslim Kaaba— ordained by Allah as the center toward which all Muslims should face every day in prayer and to which all should make a holy pilgrimage sometime in their life—becomes seen as participating in the history of the human experience of space and world construction rather than construed as an aberrantly literal geographic idea. The same goes for Christian assertions about the Church of the Holy Sepulcher in Jerusalem or traditional Chinese and Babylonian language about the imperial capital as the supreme, immovable link between heaven and earth. In some traditions the symbolism of the *axis mundi* has even been internalized, as in yogic systems where the spine is identified with a kind of microcosmic tree of life that links the body with all the levels of cosmic existence. Comparative perspective in this way gives context, dimensionality, and indeed a certain humanity, to particular histories and traditions. It creates a certain familiarity with worlds that might otherwise have been relegated to the foreign, the inferior, the bizarre. Far from ignoring history, comparative understanding here gives generic depth to it.

Understanding Context

The importance of understanding religious phenomena within their own world is another affirmation of modern comparative religion. Premodern interpreters assumed the reality of just one world, their own, and were obliged to judge all other worlds in terms of it. But a few historians such as Johann Gottfried von Herder (1744–1803) began to shake off this pattern. For Herder, each *Volk* (people or nation) had its own distinctive *Klima* (habitat or world). "In broad acceptance of the infinite variety of human cultures," Frank Manuel summarizes, "Herder broke out of traditional religious and political molds that had confined Christian Europeans for centuries."[13] But the idea took a long time to become assimilated into religious studies.

Whatever religious phenomena mean to us as interpreters, there is also the primary datum of what they signify to the adherent. Religion is always the religion *of* someone. Much confusion has come from failing to distinguish between what religion means to its participants and what it means to the outsider. Both van der Leeuw and Eliade have been criticized for not paying enough attention to what symbols mean to actual people.[14]

This point is more forcefully evident when dealing with living religions. Early comparative religion tended to deal with religion through texts, not life worlds. Understanding other people was not its concern. But the anthropologist, as Malinowski said, has "the myth-maker at his elbow," and is scientifically obligated to understand others' worlds in their own living terms. By reporting on the "insider's" or informant's view of the world, the anthropological study of religion has made a great contribution to religious studies.

The historians of religion who have contributed the most to this principle of understanding the insider's viewpoint have been those such as Wilfred Cantwell Smith who have worked in locations where European religious premises could not be taken for granted.[15] Smith also stands in the tradition of the philosopher Wilhelm Dilthey (1833–1911), who showed systematically that knowledge in the humanities generally meant "understanding" *(Verstehen)*, as opposed to "explaining," the experience of others. To see that there is nothing religious apart from religious people, and to see therefore that what religious things "are" is precisely what they *mean* to those people, is to follow a descriptive way that is at once scientific, because it is accurate and truly objective, and humanistic, because it requires engaged understanding of the positions of others.

During the centuries when xenophobia and exoticism were standard modes of relating to outsiders, the concept of understanding others and otherness was a long time in coming. Max Müller regarded the issue as a matter of justice. From the podium of the Royal Institution in 1870, he declared;

> No judge, if he had before him the worst of criminals, would treat him as most historians and theologians have treated the religions of the world. Every act in the lives of their founders, which shows that they were but men, is eagerly seized and judged without mercy; every doctrine that is not carefully guarded is interpreted in the worst sense that it will bear; every act of worship that differs from our own way of serving God is held up to ridicule and contempt. And this is not done by accident, but with a set purpose, nay, with something of that artificial sense of duty which stimulates the counsel for the defense to see nothing but an angel in one client, and anything but an angel in the plaintiff on the other side. The result has been—as it could not be otherwise—a complete miscarriage of justice, an utter misapprehension of the real character and purpose of the ancient religions of mankind.[16]

We still have a long way to go in learning how to incorporate into practice the working distinction between what religion means in its own world and what it means in the interpreter's world.

The Religious Dimension

What is it that makes anything religious? What defines the range of material to be included in religious studies? What is the unity of the subject matter? What is it that comparative religion compares? A field of religion would not even be necessary if its data could all be understood fully in terms of the methods of history, sociology, or geography. What is irreducibly religious about the subject matter that it requires special categories of study?

The premise of the study of religion is that its subject matter constitutes a special kind of phenomena, a special kind of experience, a special kind of system positing its own kind of world. In this, religion is like the arts, which also are not reducible to sociology and which also create their own frame of reference. In the face of the persistent attempt of the social sciences to explain religion in other than religious terms, it needed to be shown that religious phenomena, at least at the descriptive level, have their own content or meaning.

We need not rehearse all the ways religion has been defined by comparativists, but there has been a certain working consensus that religion is the expression in actions and representations of the sacred or holy. From the turn-of-the-century interest in "mana," as a kind of rudimentary version of the sacred,[17] to Eliade's writings, the concept of the sacred became the primary category for defining the irreducible character of religious life. There were many versions of this, but two remain classics. Rudolf Otto's *Idea of the Holy* (1917)[18] became the standard description of the experience of the holy as "the wholly Other," the mysterious reality and power that is awesome and attracting, yet also daunting. Otto labeled this "the sense of the numinous." But also influential has been Emile Durkheim's *Elementary Forms of the Religious Life* (1912),[19] which focused not on the sacred as a sense of the supernatural but on the function of the sacred in shaping collective worlds and ritual behavior. Durkheim argued that not all religions have a notion of divinity (e.g., Buddhism) but all religions do constitute communities for which there are sacred things—whether embodied in special objects, rites, principles, revered humans, or deities—and all groups oblige their membership to conduct themselves in a sacred way in relation to those sacred things.

Stress may be placed on the sacred's numinousness (Otto), inviolability (Durkheim), power (van der Leeuw), or paradigmatic function (Eliade). Or the sacred may be conceived as that object to which religious consciousness responds or as the value placed on objects and acts by humans. But religious behavior is in any case that which is founded on the distinction of sacred and profane experience. The nonreligious person, conversely, is the one for whom there is nothing sacred or holy.

The sacred has its own language. It is not the language of science but the language of myth and ritual. As such, these forms of expression are not something archaic that preceded an age of rational language, but the inherent ways the holy takes expression at all times and places. We could study the entire history of religion, but if we could not decipher the "language" of religion we would have no real context for reading that history, regardless of how much Chinese, Greek, or Sanskrit we knew. As much as any other factor, the understanding of religion is connected with the understanding of its own syntax.

The comparative study of religion has gone through several stages and is still developing. It has worked itself out according to the needs and challenges of the times. When faced with the alternatives of dogma or science, it went with science. When faced with the chaos of new data, it produced inventories and classifications. When faced by those who thought religion was only historical, it produced thematic perspective, but whenever necessary (such as when typologizing became too ungrounded) it sought out the historical, cultural, and psychological contexts of religion. Yet again, when faced with threats of reductionism, it defended the special categorical nature of the experience of the sacred. The comparative study of religion has shown its capacities for readjustment and self-correction, and there are indications that it is continuing to develop with the intellectual challenges of new times.[20]

3

Worlds

WE have presented the context of this study. It is time now to come directly to our main interpretive categories. We begin with a focused look at the concept of "world."[1] This short but pivotal chapter examines the idea of the plurality of "worlds" as a foundation and matrix for comparative study. The importance of individual context and the presence of cross-cultural patterns are both acknowledged in this category: world building is at once the specific activity that makes us different and the common activity that links us with humanity.

Religions do not all inhabit the same world, but actually posit, structure, and dwell within a universe that is their own. They can be understood not just as so many attempts to explain some common, objectively available order of things that is "out there," but as traditions that create and occupy their own universe. Acknowledging these differences in place, these intrinsically different systems of experiencing and living in the world, is fundamental to the study of religion.

The Plurality of Worlds

The idea of the plurality of worlds is one that may not come naturally. To many moderns, the globalization of secular, media-oriented culture gives the appearance of one shared world. We think we know what *the* world is. We see it as something "there," to be accepted, rather than as a product of human activity. We judge other behavior and belief in terms of what they represent within *our* system. How Christian, rationalist, and universalist worldviews accomplish this has been described above: all the different religions get construed in terms of one ideological universe. But these pictures of the world are themselves worldviews.

Our language also acknowledges the pluralistic nature of world. Ordinary speech recognizes the intrinsic diversity of spheres of life in phrases such as "the world of the Middle Ages," the "world of the honeybee," "the world of Mozart," "the world of the bedouin," or "he's in his own world." This usage, which is not merely figurative, brings out the correlation of world with relative domains. Even the etymology of the English word *world* is "the age of man,"[2] presumably in distinction to the age of the gods. The term therefore contains a strictly descriptive, relativistic value. For comparative perspective, here is an apt semantic lead.

In the broadest sense there are as many worlds as there are species; all living things select and sense "the way things are" through their own organs and modes of activity. They constellate the environment in terms of their own needs, sensory system, and values. They see—or smell or feel—what they need to, and everything else may as well not exist. A world, of whatever set of creatures, is defined by this double process of selection and exclusion.

In referring to "the world of the honeybee," no judgment is made about whether or not the bee's world exists merely in its own mind. Its world is not something that is usefully labeled true or false. A world is one's environment—the unity of existence and place—and the reality that appears to the bee is what it is relative to what the bee is and does. This use of the concept "world" thus describes versions of life space without reducing those versions to an independent norm.

In this idea of multiple worlds we find a conceptual model that represents a converging point for several modern streams of thought. The concept of world construction derives partly from the tradition of the philosopher Immanuel Kant (1724–1804), who described how the mind and its categories are the factors that structure reality. The idea that the world is not just something ready-made out there that humans passively receive or discover, but rather something that humans actively help create, is an idea that has unfolded with fascinating applications and developments in modern thought. Sociologists in the tradition of Emile Durkheim (1859–1917) have shown the correlation between social structures and cosmological, religious structures. Field anthropologists have made an industry out of describing the detailed, culture-specific nature of worlds. Philosophers of language have shown how language in all its varieties and kinds of symbols (e.g., art, myth, science) becomes not just a naming or labeling of reality but a great producer or instrument of it.[3] Philosophical phenomenology has given us the concept of the "life world" and much sophisticated analysis of the way consciousness and objects are mutually constitutive.[4] Historians of culture investigate ways that different periods and social classes shape the world according to their special configuration of values, power relationships, and knowledge.[5]

Human cultures construct an enormous variety of environments through language, technology, and institutions. We are born and die in these systems of symbols and imagination. Among these forms, religion in particular is a great definer and generator of worlds and alternative worlds.

Understanding Religious Worlds

Against the backdrop of this general idea of the relativity of life worlds, we now examine more specifically how the concept of world guides and illumines the study of religion. Our concern here is not with the worlds of molecules or interest rates but with the worlds of the sacred. There are at least a dozen specific ways the notion of plural worlds gives intelligibility to the subject matter of comparative religion.

1. Religions create, maintain, and oppose worlds. Their mythic symbols declare what the world is based on, what its oppositional forces are, what hidden worlds lie beyond or within ordinary life. The religious imagination has inexhaustibly produced ontologies of what the ancient Hindu texts

called "all this." The sacred and the real are correlative—a major point of Mircea Eliade. It is of the very essence of religion to interpret the world.

2. The notion of different worlds is an essential part of the concept and practice of "understanding others." The latter requires seeing the parts of another world in terms of the whole of that world. Everything that others do has its meaning for them within a matrix. Understanding others therefore means seeing their expressions from precisely within the perspective of their own location. In this regard, comparative religion students may be advised, "Don't worry about whether other people's beliefs and acts refer to something real in *your* world, but first understand what the beliefs and acts invoke as real in *their* world." It is the crucial difference between an insider's and an outsider's perspective, between discovering the meanings in the other world and imposing meanings from ours.

3. The idea of world helps mediate the ideas of difference and commonality. In spite of their differences, religious worlds have in common certain general forms of mythic and ritual behavior, behavior that forms the main subject matter of this study. The *content* of this behavior is always specific and historical. But the *form* of the behavior shows typical cross-cultural categories at work such as myth and ritual. We will see how it is the very nature and function of these categories to structure and express specific worlds. Religious language and behavior are not just beliefs and acts *about* the world, but actual ways through which a world comes into being. So the idea of worlds deals with the realm of particular historical matrices, yet also allows us to see typical or analogous ways by which worlds are constructed.

4. The notion of world brings out the importance of the social or collective boundaries of religion. The sociology of religion plays an important role in our understanding of world definition. Worlds are formed, held together, broken down, and re-formed by sets of people or social institutions. These sets of people give enduring plausibility to a world.[6] Being in a world is like possessing a citizenship. Worlds are not maintained by pure ideas but by actual communities that commit themselves to those ideas through socialization processes. Collectivities great or small, tribal or imperial, public or monastic,

sectarian or grandly ecclesiastical, set the terms of religious roles and identities. Myth and ritual are themselves sustained by the force of sacred collective tradition—by inviolable linkages with kinship, ancestries, brotherhoods, and sisterhoods. The power of the sacred is constantly renewed in community gatherings, and the sanctity of moral codes is given weight by the venerableness of group traditions. One swears by the god of one's tribe. One maintains the honor of one's people. The community and its authority structure is in this sense an important medium of the sacred and gives external, public "reality" to it. By the same token, when the magical coherence of collective authority is broken, so too is the sacred universe its integrity once held together.

5. The notion of world calls attention to the radical cultural and geographic diversity both among and within religious systems. To say that world definition is what religion is "about" is to hypothesize a concept that will not be subverted—as are so many theories of religion—by the sheer, endless variety of human environments that have existed cheek by jowl in religious history: hunting worlds; planting worlds; urban and rural worlds; hieratic, democratic, and portable worlds; worlds defined by oral expression, and worlds defined by writing and scripture; worlds based on physical territory, and worlds generated from internal states of consciousness. Religious universes are fashioned out of the stuff of these locations. If life is governed by cattle herding, the religious system will naturally reflect this.

6. Religious worlds can vary with differences of social position within a society. The sociologist Max Weber (1864–1920) opened up the programmatic possibilities of studying the religious attitudes of such different classes as peasants, intelligentsia, capitalists, warriors, and the underprivileged.[7] What salvation means will vary according to one's situation in society and the social values that one's location engenders. Religious symbols do not mean the same thing to the knight and the bureaucrat, the rich and the dispossessed. Social position influences the degree of worldliness or other-worldliness, the focus of ethical behavior, and the institutional forms religion will take. Where privileged classes use religion to legitimize their own life pattern and place in the world, the

particular need of the disprivileged is release from suffering, future compensation, and salvation.

In the past few years, scholars have begun to examine the effect of gender in religious experience and symbolization.[8] To Christian women, for example, the experience of a male savior sent by God the Father may be quite different from a male Christian's perception of the same symbol. A Confucian woman has entirely different obligations than her male counterpart; she is expected to imitate the "lowly, nurturing earth," as he the active, strong force of heaven. Concepts of purity vary with gender; and one's ritual domain, as in orthodox Judaism, is often determined by sex roles.

7. The concept of world underscores how language organizes reality. A religion's great powers of linguistic classification and ordering can therefore be more clearly exposed. Language—and in this case religious language—both screens and "mints" the world, determining what entities will and will not come into being. Cultures—and religious cultures—will have many and finely shaded words for the things that are important to them, no words for things totally out of their ken, and often negative words for things that threaten or defy the taxonomic system. If we live in a culture where there are only two known kinds of animals, dogs and cats, then any elephants and zebras that come into our realm might well be construed as anomalous canines or felines—or as just "odd animals." They would not exist as what they are, elephants and zebras. In the same way, we have seen how all religions other than Judaism, Christianity, and Islam have been simply labeled "paganism," the word for everything outside monotheism. In such a limited lexicon, Buddhism is unintelligible. It cannot even exist.

8. The notion of world helps make sense of the way a religious system deals with change and challenge. A world must either integrate or interpret new events. Religions are not just static systems fixed once and for all, but continually interact with changes and reshape themselves accordingly. They are like living organisms that have the autonomous capacity to learn, respond to, and control their destiny. There is a constant interplay between world and experience, between religious "program" and historical events. A world is an open,

not a closed, system, since it progresses in exchange with its environment and transforms itself accordingly. Feminist Christian theology, for instance, has not only altered the language of the liturgy but is radically changing the conception of God.

9. The concept of world provides a unifying conceptual framework for integrating the otherwise disparate contributions of many social science disciplines. Religionists have often operated in isolation from other kinds of humanistic scholarship. But any religious world is also a historical, social, and geographic world. Some theories of religion have not been able to accommodate the knowledge and perspectives created by these areas. They have imagined that one needed to choose between "religious" explanations, on the one hand, and "nonreligious" explanations, on the other. The result is often an image of religion that is quite disembodied and locationless. But modern comparative religion does not need to make such a choice. Precisely because it is concerned with religious worlds, it is obliged to deal with a rounded knowledge of place and context when attempting to understand any given religious position. Religious practices have social and psychological locations.

10. The notion of world helps avoid the distortions of intellectualizing tendencies in the interpretation of religion. As we have seen, a religious world is an inhabited place, and not reducible to just a matter of doctrine or belief. This is why philosophical arguments about deity have had so little bearing on religious life. A religious world is something lived in, acted out, embodied. It is not just disembodied minds thinking propositions about God. The concept of world is explicitly holistic. As such, it replaces classical explanatory models that pictured humans as primarily cognitive beings, and religions, accordingly, as so many sets of beliefs. In fuller perspective, religious persons are actors who express what is sacred in a huge variety of behavioral modes. World—and specifically a religious world—is thus embodied not just in the history of doctrine and religious philosophies, but in all kinds of actions and settings, such as festivals and anniversaries, passage rites, diaries, forms of self-discipline, domestic *sacra*, images and icons, special clothing and symbolic objects, techniques of healing and prayer, hymns and religious music, and innumerable local,

family, and national customs. There is an intimacy to religious practice here that needs more attention from students of the subject.[9]

11. Highly important is that the notion of world is relatively value-free and philosophically neutral with regard to a traditional dispute that has dichotomized theory for years: Is religion human-made, or is it divinely revealed? Now, insofar as the comparative study of religious worlds really sticks to descriptive and comparative understanding, the question loses relevance. It is possible to describe someone's world and its operating premises and categories without infiltrating that description with causal theories about whether that world is created by human projection or by divine revelation. In this way the term *world* is as metaphysically innocent as the term *system*.

12. Finally, the concept of world shows that interpretations of religion are themselves products of worlds. For example, the issue of natural versus supernatural "explanation" is not something that admits to any objective resolution, since whatever position one takes is itself an instance and enactment of a worldview. Ideas about "natural" explanation or "human projections" are categories of secular worldviews. Ideas of divine revelation are categories of those inhabiting theistic universes. The way one explains the world is itself a linguistic manifestation of the kind of world in which the explainer dwells.

Types of Religious Worlds

The way one classifies different types of religious worlds also reflects the classifier's own purposes. For some, the different types of religious worlds are simply the different religions themselves. Texts on world religions reflect this approach. For others, the different types of religious worlds are placed on an evolutionary line beginning with the spiritually "lower" types and leading up to the spiritually "higher" types. The schema gets filled out according to one's preferred philosophy of life.

A strictly sociological typology popular in Western religious scholarship differentiates between "church" and "sect" as two kinds of religious communities. It is a typology that has helped explain the diversity of Western religion. In the most general terms, a church is the established religion of a society, whereas a sect is a small, voluntary association, with a high level of commitment and strong, authoritative leadership. The sect maintains strict boundaries between itself and others. Most modern religions began as sects. Where sects survive the first generation of membership, they tend to take on the features of churches. Some would go further and distinguish between sects and cults, the former being considered separatist versions of the dominant churches (e.g., the Amish or Jehovah's Witnesses) and the latter being small groups geared toward inner spiritual fulfilment with little relation to historical society at all (e.g., Theosophy, Self-Realization Fellowship, and other Asian-based, meditation-centered groups). The distinctions are Western. In broader, non-Western perspective we must admit that there are nearly as many kinds of religious institutions as there are kinds of communities and subcommunities.

More germane to our theme is to look at kinds of religious worlds in terms of the types of things that form their sacred focus. This follows from the hypothesis that the sacred defines the world. We therefore ask of any given system, "Where is the sacred?"

For one class of religion, the sacred is environmental. It is connected with physical location. It may be related to powers that rule the hunt, or that govern the fertility of the herds or crops, or that maintain kinship unity and clan survival. It may be found in the realms of health, political power, and local ancestry.

Distinctly different from these "environmental" religions are those systems focusing on self-transformation and self-transcendence. This is the type exemplified by transethnic systems such as Buddhism and Christianity, with their ideals of liberating the individual—whatever the tribe or location—from the profanity within. Holiness here is not a geographical or social force but is connected with ego transcendence. Once ideals of self-perfection come into play, all kinds of new re-

ligious possibilities arise. Is holiness the perfection of love?
Wisdom? How is it related to one's behavior toward other
people? How can it be integrated with ordinary life and
activity?

The study of the locations of the sacred is a study in the
varieties of things that sustain human life and the concomitant
variety of things that profane or destroy life. Where life is
local, the sacred and the profane will be local. Where life
is individual, the sacred and the profane will be individual.
Where life is institutional or cultic, so the sacred/profane distinction follows suit. Before the rise of religions calling for
salvation *from* the world, religion was based on place—for
instance, one's forest, one's gardening fields, or one's city-
state. Stone Age Australian aboriginal religion is based almost
entirely on a relationship to the immediate landscape, which
is construed as being marked by various "actions" of the ancestors. With the coming of religions of individual transformation
came a new location, a new territory of concern: the interior
self.

Worlds at Stake: Maintenance, Interaction, Change

The nature of religious worlds is brought out most vividly in
times of crisis. Systems are exposed and at stake when boundaries are challenged or when violation takes place. The history
of religions shows not just a set of fixed, eternal worlds, but
also constant tolerance testing. It is a history of worlds in
conflict and worlds undergoing their own life cycles of creation, destruction, re-formation.

Within their own domain, religious worlds have built in
ways of dealing with normal crises. Religions are systems that
must cope with the full burden of human suffering, and affliction, disasters, and death must all be addressed by the
resources of myth, scripture, and ritual. Within its own world,
there is nothing a religion cannot explain or at least interpret.
Negative events are given meaning, rationalized, or at least
made bearable by religious justifications and prototypes.
"Blessed are those," said Jesus, "who are persecuted for righteousness' sake, for theirs is the kingdom of heaven." "Your

problems," say the gurus, "are but opportunities for more consciousness."

But there is also a different kind of threat that is more dangerous and subversive. It is the threat of *competing* worlds that challenges the very foundations of one's own. The normal round of accidents or untimely deaths is not so much what erodes systems as the presence of alternative authorities. The Holocaust was not the end of Judaism, unaccountable as the magnitude of its evil was. The Bible itself contains paradigms for inexplicable affliction (such as the experience of Job) as well as for deserved or punitive suffering (the Israelites had broken God's laws and hence were punished and dispersed by the Assyrian armies). In an anguishing way, the Holocaust seemed not anomalous with the history of Jewish suffering and persecution. Ironically, Judaism per se has been threatened much more by the competitive, erosive threat of secular cultural systems and boundary-dissolving intermarriages.

If the sacred is the foundation of a world, then whatever denies that sacredness will be intolerable. Sometimes the threat comes from inside a religion in the form of heresies or violations of authority. Worlds are most threatened by those close enough to usurp the system.[10] The history of religious exclusivity and punishment show the dramatic importance of these threats and the urgency of maintaining order. What offends that sacred order gets purged, destroyed, or expelled. Such has been the story of interreligious wars, the fate of minorities, the chilling sacrifice of "the other" to the survival of "one's own."[11] The noblest ethical teachings have been quickly forgotten when territory is at stake.

We have seen how the very existence of other religions was a standing offense to many traditional Christians. But in modern times it is often secular people who have felt threatened by the so-called cults. And now, in turn, "secular humanism" appears as a demonic competitor to fundamentalist religion.

Another way of analyzing world boundaries is in terms of how religions handle secularization and social change. There are four typical kinds of religious responses to such changes.

The first is the conservative response of tightening up, solidifying, and defending boundaries. In the face of chaos, religion here contracts to save its life. Fundamentalism, found in all historical religions, is just one of the names for this stance that retreats to the absolute authority of its faith and thereby thickens its insulation from competition. Rigorous self-definition is expressed and insisted on in creeds and conduct. The words of scripture are taken as the infallible, absolute words of God, daunting and inexplicable to the worldly minded. Relativism is abhorrent. Religion is to be recovered in its uncompromising pure form, insusceptible to worldly, human corruption or "liberal" interpretation.

The second response to modernity is accommodation or religious liberalism. This, too, is found in all historical religions that have confronted different or secular cultures. Religion is adapted to coexist with new values. Where the conservative takes an either-or stance (e.g., either the Bible or "the world"), the liberal accommodates both old and new. Modern religious life often blends secular styles and traditional symbols in a way that is almost inconspicuous, so much so that we might be scarcely aware of the finesse with which one world, out of two different worlds, is being blended and expressed before our eyes. Christmas and Easter celebrations visibly show such a joining of secular and religious value systems.

The third possibility of world formation is association with new religious groups. Sometimes there is no hope for reviving an old tradition. A clean break, a fresh start is seen as the alternative, and this happens with regularity in changing cultures. The old spaces become unlivable. Old systems become irrelevant, suspect, corrupt, without authority. The thousands of new religious movements today are like so many new worlds, alternative to those that have worn out in twentieth-century processes of social change. Every day before our eyes we see new religious systems move in to fill the space, to create or re-create new authority and norms, to divulge new revelations or myths, to reconstruct roots and identity. The phenomenon has produced one of the liveliest, most expansive areas of research in the study of religion.[12]

New forms of religious life might well be regarded with the same respect a biologist would have for a newly identified species. A new religion is a unique, self-contained adaptation to the environment, and that adaptation is often a specific compensatory movement supplying a form of spirituality that has been lacking. These groups reconstruct social existence around forms of community that are more satisfying than what ordinary life offers. Monasteries, utopian experiments, small spiritual "families," and secret brotherhoods and sisterhoods meet this need. New groups reconstruct ethnic existence around systems of revitalization and dignity, which give esteem and divinely sanctioned "place" to those who have been oppressed. They reconstruct individual consciousness by supplying regimens of self-improvement, as well as role models in the form of charismatic teachers who embody the new ideal. Revivalist missions and television ministries reconstruct the worlds of the "sinner," the ill, and the estranged, offering resources of power beyond the individual's own. Many are the lost who find clarity and explanatory power in the theologies of the new prophets. Many are those who seek ecstatic contact with power in a powerless, impersonal world, and find direct, experiential manifestation of this energetic spirit in pentecostal or charismatic groups.

The enormous variety of new religions shows the dynamic character of world building and reveals an almost incomprehensible, teeming diversity of coexisting worlds. There are more than 10,000 new religious movements in black Africa today. Each has its "myth," typically a syncretistic combination of native and Islamic or Christian worlds. Countless new religions also flourish in countries such as Japan and America, offering new livelihood to the spiritually uprooted citizenries of urban populations.[13]

But there is a revealing factor about these new groups. More often than not the "new" systems present themselves as a recovery or restoration of something old. They offer a new understanding of ancient or lost truths. They revitalize life by revitalizing myth. For instance, a multitude of "neo-pagan" and feminist groups have revived goddess worship.[14]

The fourth religious response to modernity is individualism. Here too is a world, a place. Spirituality becomes privatized and self-styled. So prevalent, unobtrusive, and taken for granted is this individualism that we are apt not even to include it in the study of religion. One report submits this illustration:

Today religion in America is as private and diverse as New England colonial religion was public and unified. One person we interviewed has actually named her religion (she calls it her "faith") after herself. This suggests the logical possibility of over 220 million American religions, one for each of us. Sheila Larson is a young nurse who has received a good deal of therapy and who describes her faith as "Sheilaism." "I believe in God. I'm not a religious fanatic. I can't remember the last time I went to church. My faith has carried me a long way. It's Sheilaism. Just my own little voice." Sheila's faith has some tenets beyond belief in God, though not many. In defining "my own Sheilaism," she said: It's just try to love yourself and be gentle with yourself. You know, I guess, take care of each other. I think He would want us to take care of each other."[15]

Not all individual religion is so patently self-styled, but it is characterized by the construction of a world around highly personal values—around "what works for me."

How can we understand what is other? How can we know something if there is nothing in our experience to relate it to? How can Columbus "know" a wholly new continent other than through his own projected categories? How can a Christian fundamentalist "know" the world of a Buddhist monk or an Asian guru? How can we understand all the things religious worlds can be?

Understanding is possible in principle because, in spite of otherness, there is also commonality. No religious culture is so totally unique as to defy outside comprehension. We can begin to understand others through those categories that bridge religious worlds. The comparative framework outlined in the following chapters will identify some such common forms, while trying to describe these structures in a way that is not too preemptively ethnocentric.

The fundamental bridging category is "world." It is the common denominator that grounds other comparative concepts. Because different worlds are versions of world making, it is possible in principle to understand them, just as one might learn a new program, a new game, or a new language if one understood the *idea* of a program, a game, or a language. No matter how much otherness the world of the "other" has, it is, after all, one human system alongside others, a *type* of world, with its own sacred things. To understand it as such is the first act of comparative perspective.

Part Two

Structures and Variations in Religious Worlds

4

Myth

THE language of religion is different than the language of
science. Scientific discourse aspires to objectivity, but religious
symbols are by nature participatory, enactive, involving. Religious systems are always grounded in authoritative accounts
of great foundational forces that generate and govern the
world. To the participant, these are not just poetic or rationalistic speculations about the universe, but sacred words and
models by which one lives. Religious life constantly refers itself
to the truth of these models and to the beings and objects that
embody them. The generic term used here for such grounding
prototypes, whether embodied in the sacred stories of oral
cultures or in the scriptures of historical religions, is *myth.*

Because the word *myth* has various interpretations and is
employed in diverse contexts,[1] we will first need to back up
a little and see how its use as "the world-building, world-
shaping language of religion" can be justified.

Myth: Approaching the Term

From ancient Greek times the term *myth* has had both positive
and negative uses. The ambivalence developed for reasons
partly semantic and partly attitudinal. The Greek *mythos* orig-

inally meant anything delivered by word of mouth, such as a statement, an order, a speech, or a story. In its broadest sense the term meant "word" or "speech." Homer used *mythos* in contraposition to *ergon,* deed. But in time another contrast took place. *Mythos* came to be contrasted with other modes of discourse. Gradually, as one historian sums up this development, "*mythos* became the word as the most ancient, the original account of the origins of the world, in divine revelation or sacred tradition, of gods and demigods and the genesis of the cosmos, cosmogony; and it came to be sharply contrasted with *epos,* the word as human narration, and—from the Sophists on—with *logos,* the word as rational construction."[2] Hence, whereas Greek philosophers construed myth to mean a fanciful tale as opposed to true, discursive language, others took *myth* as the word that conveys an original, primal state of things, as opposed to merely superficial, human words.

These two different uses of the term are still current. In relation to discursive language, myth can appear as either merely imaginary or as profoundly true, something that is less than factual or something that is sublimely transrational. Some do indeed equate myth and fantasy, whereas others see myth, or "mythopoetic language," as a vehicle of deeper truths than those conveyed by scientific, denotative discourse. Several philosophers of the romantic period were vigorous exponents of the latter approach.[3]

In current Western culture the word myth is often used in a negative sense. This reflects the outlook of biblical religion but also of some strands of Western rationalism and literature. The New Testament contrasted the "vanity" of myths with the truth of the Gospel.[4] Scientific culture for its part tends to see mythology as an archaic, "prelogical" stage of human cognition. Literature usually takes myth as an early genre of storytelling that preceded the emergence of the modern epic and other narrative forms. Western readers who have formed their idea of myth from Greek literature naturally conclude that the word refers to fantastic, entertaining stories about gods and heroes. For many people, myth is simply the realm of imagination, the domain of centaurs, unicorns, and miracles. And current colloquial style often uses the term *myth* to mean any belief that is given uncritical acceptance, so that we have phrases such as "myths of racial superiority" or "ten myths about cancer."

But the study of religion requires a different, more positive use of the term, corresponding to the actual function of mythic language within living religious contexts.

Fieldwork anthropologists such as Bronislaw Malinowski discovered that in tribal societies myth is

> not merely a story told, but a reality lived. It is not of the nature of fiction, such as we read today in novels, but it is a living reality, believed to have once happened in primeval times, and continuing ever since to influence the world and human destinies. This myth is to the savage what, to a fully believing Christian, is the Biblical story of Creation, of the Fall, of the Redemption by Christ's Sacrifice on the cross. As our sacred story lives in our ritual, in our morality, as it governs our faith and controls our conduct, even so does his myth for the savage.[5]

In addition, anthropologists found within the settings of tribal life that these communities had clear distinctions between stories of entertainment and sacred stories that defined the normative precedents by which their behavior was guided and on which their universe was founded. The Pawnee Indians refer to these two types in their distinction of "false stories" and "true stories." The Eskimos acknowledge a difference between "young stories" and "old stories," and the Winnebago classification is "narrated" versus "sacred" accounts. The study of living cultures therefore showed that myth referred not just to the residue of what people no longer believe, but to the operating "constitution" or "charter" of a people's moral, social, and metaphysical existence. Anthropologists, in short, took the emphasis away from contextless Greek texts, put the mythmaker back in the picture, and discovered an intrinsic connection between myth and the life world. Myth could no longer simply be equated with Greek tales about the loves of Zeus.

Mircea Eliade's work provided an extensive development of this positive revalorization of the concept of myth. Eliade stressed the paradigmatic or "contemporary" functions of myth, particularly cosmogonic (world-creating) myths. His focus was on the religious rather than sociological function of myth and his prototype the Australian aborigines' concept of the "Dreamtime" (the *Alcheringa*), a "Great Time" that is chronologically ambiguous but that constitutes a living landscape of sacred ancestors and their great deeds. Through ritual and holy songs, tribe members periodically make themselves contemporary with that "history," reenacting the events of "that time." Eliade's emphasis on mythic time as the source of creative power amounted to a recovery of the idea of *mythos* as primal or original "word." His emphasis on the sacred function of myth opened up new avenues of interpreting the general history of religions.

The sacred, prototypical function of myth distinguishes it from other genres of narrative. For example, myth is essentially different from folktales that tell of a make-believe realm set in a nonexistent time and place with deliberately fictive characters. Rather, myth posits ostensibly real times and places, real heroes and ancestors, real genealogies and events. No matter how imaginative these may seem to an outsider, mythic settings are intended by the believers to represent an account of the actual world. In contrast, the folktale aims at entertainment and is not at all authoritative. As one commentator puts it well, "Whereas the typical fairy tale opens with: 'Once upon a time . . . ,' the typical myth begins with: 'In the beginning . . .' "[6]

Another type of story, the etiological tale, is also different in purpose from myth. Etiologies (from *aitia*, cause) simply and literally aim at explaining why a particular thing came to be the way it is. For example, the shape of a particular mountain may be said to have received its special form from the way a primordial ancestor reclined on it. Such stories are versions of the "how the elephant got its trunk" genre. They are explanations transparently made up after the fact, and their sole intention is explanation. Many etiologies become parts of mythological canons and serve some mythic function. Yet myth per se does not deal with the merely technical question of how things came into existence, but exposits the overall sacred purposes and values of things.

Some sagas, epics, and legends have a mythic dimension in that they deal with a "real," rather than imaginary, past. They may tell of great heroes, ancestors, and saints. They may have a prototypical function by featuring inspiring models of great deeds and virtues. Certainly the much-venerated Homeric and Hindu epics achieved a mythic prestige. Yet in general, epics tend not to deal with the ultimate foundations of the world as myth does. In fact, they usually presuppose myth, amplifying it at the popular, quasi-historical level.

Myth and Religion

We may now expand on our initial, summary characterization of myth.

Religions are grounded in mythic language. In its most fundamental function this language gives an account of that on which the world is based. It names the powers and principles that create and govern the world. It is language that has a given, primordial character. Myth is not a medium of neutral, mathematical objectivity, but a definitive voice that names the ultimate powers that create, maintain, and re-create one's life. It is a voice that articulates the prototypical events—such as the Creation, the Resurrection, the Enlightenment of the Buddha—beings, and teachings that form the standards for all subsequent religious life. These foundational realities may be conceived as prehistorical, historical, or heavenly, but they always have an eternal, exemplary nature. Hence, the power of religious myth is best illustrated not in children's stories about defunct Greek gods, but in the living scriptures and gods of living religions. Fictions only to the outsider, myth to the insider is text and program. In biblical cultures, scripture is myth, and *God* is the mythic word par excellence.

Within religious worlds, myth is not solely a matter of representation. It is not just a language "about" something. It is always paradigmatic, authoritative, applicable. It is often enacted in behavior and ritual. Myth as world script not only explains the world but also constructs and governs it. Stories that simply spin imaginative accounts of supernatural beings but that have no sacred status and force for defining human behavior are just folktales.

As a term for understanding other worlds, *myth* is an alternative to *belief*. We are used to explaining religions in terms of their doctrines or convictions. But "belief" describes religion

in terms of a fairly narrow, one-way cognitive street, empha-
sizing just human ideas *about* something out there. Myth, on
the other hand, suggests that religious language is experienced
not simply as our own projection or instrumentality but as a
worldview and semantic matrix in its own right, organizing
and presenting reality in a way that makes humans not just
conceivers but respondents and partakers. Myth is a phenomenological concept that brings out the two-way character of
language and links—as the term *belief* does not—the concepts
of language and world.

It follows that not every account of origins is mythic.
Science accounts for origins, but only in rare cases might it
function as myth. Modern theories of the physical origin of
the universe and life are not myths to be enacted but hypotheses to be tested. Detached, purely empirical and theoretical, they are neutral of any human or ritual involvement.
But religious myth is by definition something that engages us.
It is a source for healing, restoration, liberation, order, power,
salvation. It underlies the sanctity of important moral choices.
One does not take oaths on the big bang literature, resort to
The Origin of the Species in times of crisis, or perform daily
observances for the founding role of amino acids in the creation
and sustenance of life.

Myth not only supplies precedents and norms but actually
recreates or transfigures life in its image. For example, faith
in God—and gods are living pieces of myth—creates a different way of experiencing everyday life than without such
faith.

In this perspective, myth is a category that is applicable
to all religion and not just nonbiblical religion. In contrast
with scientific language, all religious language is mythic. The
concept of myth helps overcome the insidious bifurcation of
religious language into the "beliefs" of the higher religions and
the "myths" of primitive (or pagan) religions. To distinguish
the mythologies of other religions from the truths of one's own
may be a perfectly convenient, semantic ploy in defending a
theological position, but as a distinction in the comparative
study of religion it is distortive.

There are two levels of religious language. The first,
the voice of myth per se, undergirds the second, which

is the explications of doctrine, commentary, religious law, and theology. These are sometimes called "first-order" and "second-order" religious language. The first embodies the religious realities it signifies. It is the language of scripture and its oral equivalents. The second speaks *about* the first type of language; that is, it participates in myth but is derivative from it.

In this book, myth is viewed in religious terms, and religion in mythic terms. Myths are not represented as versions of prescientific attempts to explain the cosmos or as charming stories about the mystery of existence in general. Nor will we deal with the history of mythic symbols in order to show what they have to say about the evolution of a collective unconscious, or reduce myths to coded social symbolisms.[7] Rather, in the following sections, myth will be shown to function as a sacred, world-constituting language within living religious systems.

Myth and Time

Myth and time are related categories within a religious world. Myth circumscribes the whole of life and history—past, present, and future—and invests these categories with their meanings. Myth orders time in terms of what is timeless. Different mythologies partition and valorize time in different ways.

Each religious world has its own past. Each has its own history, its own time. In this sense there are thousands of pasts, thousands of different origins of the world, thousands of different founding events. For each tradition these origins are absolute, which is a feature of the grounding character of myth. These pasts and histories are given form not through scientific evidence but through the memory and continuity of tradition. Every past rises up around key events and exemplary figures, and it persists not because it is historiographically correct but because its symbolism embodies so perfectly the ideals and dignity of the community.

These histories are not just something "back there." They have an omnipresence. Mythic time is more than just chronological time. The primary entities of myth—such as the gods, buddhas, and ancestors—are larger than history. In traditional cultures such as those in China and Africa, the deceased do not disappear. They continue to exist as ancestors. For most Christians and Buddhists, the Christ and the Buddha are not just historical heroes who appeared, taught remarkable truths, and departed. They are the names of timeless, archetypal beings. "In the beginning was the Word . . . " starts the Gospel of John, referring to Christ, who in that same writing states, "Before Abraham was, I am."[8] The first council of Christian bishops (Nicaea, 325 C.E.) affirmed as dogma that Christ is not part of the finite, "created" world and "that there never was a time when the Son was not." Buddhist scriptures such as the popular Lotus Sutra proclaim that the real Buddha is not just the historical Gautama but an eternal being who reveals himself in countless ways throughout limitless eons. Similarly, Jews, Muslims, and Sikhs regard the Torah, the Qur'an, and the Adi Granth as the primal, contemporary, unalterable words of God. Legends tell of how the Torah existed before the Creation itself. Pious Muslims regard earthly Qur'ans as but copies of an eternal one in heaven. In this sense, myth is not just an account of what was, but an account of what is.

Myth does not always look back; there are myths of the future as well as of the past. Both kinds hold up a "Great Time" in terms of which humans are to guide their lives. The Christian Bible, for example, begins with the myth of origins but ends with the myth of the Last Judgment and coming City of God. It has even been suggested that the God of the Hebrew prophets "stands not so much at the beginning of time as at its end; he is not so much the origin of all history as its ethical and religious fulfillment."[9] Messianic traditions look forward to a savior who will redeem the faithful, and apocalyptic myths regard the present not in the light of origins but in terms of anticipated "final" events and revelations to come, such as the end of the old world, the return of the dead, a final vindicating battle, judgment of the wicked, justification of the true believers, a divinely established new world. Many traditional religions posit images of the soul's destiny in an afterlife—for instance, in heavens, purgatories, and hells. Anything that depicts forms of immortality or eternal life belongs to the realm of myth. Myth points not just to a past to be regained, but to a future life for which one must prepare.

Some mythologies view the whole of worldly time as a negative or meaningless process and describe redemption from the wheel of time as the highest human goal. Early Buddhism saw ordinary life as an endless succession of birth, death, and rebirth. The solution to this state of constant impermanence and suffering, this *samsara*, was *nirvana*, a timeless, deconditioned state achieved by discipline. For some mythologies, earth is home; for others, the "world" is a prison.

Other myths, such as in Hinduism, describe constant cycles of world creation and destruction. The world is eternally generated, run down, and regenerated. This is not necessarily a negative valuation of the world—the universe is sometimes depicted as the "play," "dance," "dream," or "inbreathing/outbreathing" of the divine being—but it is a way of saying that the religious fulfillment of life is in the ahistorical, cosmic realm, not in the domain of change or historical progress.

Myth essentially lives out of ahistorical principles, whether those principles are embodied in gods, "historical" events, or images of an enduring world harmony. Mythic order has been posited in every conceivable dimension of existence, such as numbers (numerology) and heavenly patterns (astrology). Many cultures developed mythic categories that named the ultimate force of order in the universe, such as the early Hindu *rita*, the Egyptian *maat*, the Chinese *tao* (and sometimes *tien*, heaven), and the Greek *moira*. One Persian sect honored *zurvan akarana*, "endless time," as the ultimate form of the universe itself. Often destiny or fate become important concepts, and colloquial pieties such as "Allah wills it" or "God willing" show the assimilation of fate with deity. Some mythologies developed sophisticated concepts about the whole of time as a harmony of opposites.

Some historians of religion stop short of including the Bible as "myth" because they believe that myth is transhistorical time, whereas the Bible reflects historical experience. Yet if we are to deal with the way the Bible applies to the lives of its followers, we will see that the "history" of the Bible actually *functions* as transhistorical or "great" time for its believers. It is certainly the prototypical time in which divine events and words have been definitively posited and that is renewed at every religious service and festival.

Myth and tradition are categories that overlap. They share the same authority: the absoluteness of precedent and the prestige of the past. Most religious life and ritual persists not because people "believe" in them intellectually but because "this is the way it has been done by the ancestors." Religions are communities of memory more than they are collections of dogmas. The sanctity of tradition and the sanctity of myth reinforce each other. Like myth, tradition has an obligatory givenness, presenting itself to its participants with a categorical force. It is tradition, as Tevye of *The Fiddler on the Roof* said, that "lets you know who you are and what God expects from you."

Myth, like tradition, often involves a lineage. It places humans in a chain of being. Identity is depicted through notions of spiritual ancestry and transmission, and in this regard mythology often speaks of an original relationship of humans and gods. Myth tells us what or whom we are descended from. Tribal and national mythologies typically incorporate genealogies. The framework of the Book of Genesis is largely genealogical, and the Christian New Testament begins with the lineage of Jesus, tracing his paternal side to Abraham (the Gospel of Luke traces it to Adam). It is safe to hypothesize that all traditional hieratic and imperial institutions traced the succession of their sacred leadership to original divine endowment of some kind.

Myth gives time a structure, a shape. It also shows what is timeless. It speaks of our roots and our possible destiny. It tells us where we came from, who we are, and where we are going.

The Power of the Mythic Word

Myth is not only the canopy of time but a special type of language in its own right and with its own kind of power. This power takes many forms. Myth is different in quality than everyday language, and it is not surprising that access to it often involves religious preparation or initiation. Unlike scientific language, which is value-free and informational, mythic language is a kind of agency. It is expressive, charged, resonant. It summons up and embodies the very presence of that to which it refers.

In the language of myth, all things are possible. Myth is different from the flattening, discursive language of data and systems of verifiable facts. Myth has no such limits. It is tantamount to the world of the gods, and in principle there is nothing the gods cannot do. In its elasticity, comprehensiveness, and capacity to embrace opposites, myth deals with the unlimited aspect of existence. As the historian of religion Kees Bolle has stressed, myth creates freedom from the realm of the finite, the routine, the inexorable.[10] In this particular sense, some mythic language does share qualities of other forms of imaginative or poetic speech and writing. Myth thinks in images. It has fluidity. It puts things together that ordinary logic holds apart. It exalts, idealizes, embroiders, and is still true to its nature.

Yet myth is not strictly to be equated with the realm of the fantastic or imaginative. There is much that is fantastic that is not myth and much that is myth that is not fantastic. Any linguistic model of the world that presents itself as the ultimate truth of the world and is applied to life in a sacred manner is mythic thinking. But sheer fantasy, just for the sake of fantasy, is not necessarily myth. The arts inhabit a world of images, but they are momentary images, without sustained, religious authority. It is the sacred attitude *toward* mythic words that makes them myth, not the fact that the words simply depict marvelous, supernatural events, which any folktale or film can do.

Wherever there are acts and words of gods, there is mythic language. Gods by their very nature are manifestations of myth; and monotheism, simply because it has "one" god only, is no exception. Judaism, Christianity, and Islam all make "the Word" of God the primary channel by which divinity is known to humans and by which humans can realize God, and there is no better paradigm of mythic language than the concept of the Word of God. So the Bible is not just an historical document that happens to contain a few myth fragments such as the Garden of Eden and Noah's Ark. *Whenever* a god speaks, myth is speaking. As the Gospel of Matthew declares, "Man shall not live by bread alone, but by every word that proceedeth out of the mouth of God."[11] Those who set out to demythologize the Bible by distinguishing a mythological husk from a religious nucleus overlook the point that, compared with the language of science, the Bible as a whole functions as *mythos*. The Christian gospel that God has "acted in a decisive, saving way through the event of Jesus Christ" is not some kind of nonmythic kernel surrounded by the chaff of Hellenistic mythology, but a perfect instance of the power of myth itself.

For years compilers of anthologies on "mythologies of the world" omitted any reference to the Judeo-Christian texts and traditions, presumably on the grounds that these traditions represented something on a "truer," transmythic plane. But in terms of the broader, generic character of mythic language, where myth is a paradigmatic account of the world and the sacred, the Western material must clearly be included. The Bible, like other scriptures, contains the definitive "words of life" to which all ordinary life is referred. One does not need to resort to "primitive" societies or exotic accounts of primal world eggs and androgynes in order to see myth at work. The miraculous rescue of Israel from Egypt by the "mighty hand of God" and the victorious resurrection of the Son of God defeating the powers of death are excellent examples.

Part of the power of myth is in the absolute status it is given in the form of scriptures and their oral equivalents in nonliterate cultures. Scriptures are not just collections of literature.[12] They are a canonization of immutable mythic words of any kind. The Qur'an is not a book of fabulous, miraculous histories but mostly a set of sayings and injunctions. The Vedas are collections of chants, hymns, ritual formulae, and teaching dialogues. The Western Bible is mythic not just because it tells of the incredible acts of a god but also because of the authoritative status it has as a corpus of laws, proverbs, psalms, genealogies, and prophecies. The fundamentalist who devoutly avers the absolute inerrancy of Scripture is but acting out the inherent nature of mythic authority. The "oral Torah" in Judaism, condensed in the Talmud, surrounds every syllable of scripture with commentary and interpretation. Protestant reformers made the pulpit rather than the altar the center of the church service. New religions often elevate the "inspired" words of the founder to mythic status, so that just as we witness myriads of origins of the world and centers of the world, so too do we find myriads of works that constitute "the holy text" of the world.

The holiness of mythic words is expressed in many ways. They are not simply information to be read or communicated but realities to be recited, chanted, intoned, learned. They are listened to, participated in, indulged. They are memorized. They are reached out for and held on to in times of need. Traditional education is based on them. All daily life should be lived with reference to them. All significant events are accompanied by them. The high point of the bar mitzvah and bas mitzvah ceremonies is the recitation of scripture before the congregation. The scriptural words "What God has joined together let no man put asunder" solemnizes Christian weddings.[13] Muslims perform daily prayers that begin with the opening lines of the Qur'an. Copying a Torah scroll is a holy act, and in connection with traditional liturgical ritual, its mantle is kissed by congregants. The orthodox Jewish male carries out the injunction that the words of God be "inscribed on one's heart"; he wears tefillin—small boxes containing scriptural passages—around his head and arm for appointed times of prayer. The words of canonic myth are the "water of life."

Mythic language can sometimes be focused in a powerful, concentrated way in particularly charged words, names, or phrases. Reciting a prayer, chanting a mantra, or invoking the name of a god are pure forms of direct participation in the mythic mode. The divinely ordained Lord's Prayer is for Christians an enduring set of words given as a channel between humans and "our Father in Heaven." The sacred Hindu syllable, *om*, is believed to contain the primal sound of the universe itself. The central religious act of Pure Land Buddhism is the *nembutsu,* a recitation consisting of three words, *Namu Amida Butsu* (Homage to Amida Buddha). Invoked with grateful sincerity the very act of intoning the phrase is believed to have the power to bring the devotee into total participation in the saving powers of Amida, including life in "His Pure Land." For comparative perspective, we need only think of how many millions of times the names of countless gods have been uttered in a similar spirit. In recited myth, the word *is* the thing itself. In the consciousness of participants, the mythic Word moves mountains. In traditional cultures, the names of patron gods were often kept secret so that enemies could not misuse them, the name of the gods being the god itself.

Mythic words are not limited to the voices of gods. The archetypal function of language can be effected through any authority, such as ancestors, shamans, sages, buddhas, and creeds. Buddhist *sutras* typically begin with "Thus have I heard," before going on to recount the glorious deeds and *dharma* (the true teaching) of the Buddha. Confucian writings had the function of scripture for hundreds of years in China. Though not based on any concept of divine revelation, many temples had the *Analects* inscribed on stone tablets, and the educational system required committing the entire canon to memory. It is notable that even the "little red book" of Maoism, the *Thoughts of Chairman Mao,* assumed scriptural status for a short period in the People's Republic of China.

The impressiveness of myth does not depend on the elements of deity and storytelling. Words and writings are mythic by virtue of people's attitudes toward them and the role they play in people's lives. Myth can be expressed through ahistorical images and principles. The *I Ching,* for example, has a scriptural function as a great source book of condensed archetypal images, yet it is not a story and has no historical dimension whatsoever. It is a system of cosmological images expressing different modes, situations, and permutations of nature, change, and life. It engages the participants. The principles of yin and yang here are not deities but symbols of the receiving and active forces in life, and as such ground the religious insights of this divinatory text. The Hindu image of the divine reality, Brahman, is similarly a "grounding" concept that is mythic at the core. Brahman—an early meaning was the "word of prayer"—came to designate the one great reality of which all others, including all gods and humans, are parts. Brahman is "hidden" in "all this." It is "the one thing, knowing which, all else is known." There are many similar religious philosophies—Platonism and its variants are examples—that view the universe as an eternal, preestablished state of divine being that it should be the human goal to "realize." These are therefore instances of the ahistorical, mystical forms of myth. World is named; human life is lived and fulfilled in that name.

All these examples are versions and derivations of the language of myth, and we diminish our comparative grasp of the subject if we exclude them from the spectrum. They show that the scope, style, and nature of myth mirror the scope, style, and nature of many different kinds of worlds.

Myth and the Variety of Worlds

The content of myth varies with the content of worlds. Myth deals with the stuff of worlds. It grounds and elaborates in transhistorical images what is central to a world. Myth not only shapes existence; it mirrors it.

Myth deals with the "species" on which life depends. We find Eskimo myths of the origin of sea mammals, Navaho myths linking the origin of humans with the origin of corn, Babylonian myths dealing with the founding deeds of the god-king Marduk, Japanese myths dealing with prototypical episodes of purity and shame, Amazon basin myths dealing with the origin of warfare, sorcery, and psychotropic plants, and cabalistic myths dealing with the mystical exile and reunion of God and soul. Fishing culture myths tell of the first fishery, hunting culture myths of the first hunt. The pastoralist Masai, who subsist on cattle products, have a myth stating that at the beginning God created cattle for the Masai to live by, and that all the cattle in the world are theirs by divine right. Where a tribe's subsistence is bound to its specific territory, then myth will show the supernatural origin and "history" of that landscape in detail. Where world is held together by factors of lineage or social descent, myth is preoccupied with genealogy. Where authority or hierarchy rule life, as in the great city-states of the ancient world, we find myths such as the Mesopotamian *Enuma Elish* dealing with the origin and authority of divine kingship. The central Hebraic myth is that of the origins and "covenant" history of the Jewish community itself.

Myth tells of the origin of all essential skills, knowledge, and institutions. What is sacred is given mythic status. Through myth we can discover what categories are central to a world. In this way we respect accounts of how the ancestors or gods gave humans the life sustaining arts of making fire, weapons, magic, tools, canoes, and dams. Elsewhere, "essential knowledge" may be of a moral kind, with the myths focusing on the gift of religious laws. The "laws of Moses" given on Mt. Sinai—including the Ten Commandments but also cultic and civil regulations—are such a collection.

Myth also can focus on the origin of the means by which humans communicate with the gods. Shamanic cultures have myths telling of the origin of shamanism. Sometimes a sacramental object is the key to communication with the spirit world. The Plains Indians mythologize their sacred pipe—used as a medium for prayers—as having been especially given for human welfare by the Great Spirit. All individual pipes embody the one, "Original Pipe" given to the Indians by God. The Tukano Indians have an important myth about the origin of a narcotic plant, *yaje,* which is their primary means of access to the world of the spirits. The plant is represented in the story as the divinely conceived child of the "first woman in Creation," Yaje Woman. The account tells how the child was brought to a men's lodge. The Yaje Woman

> looked around and asked: "Who is the father of this child?" A man who was sitting nearby said: "I am his father!" Taking off one of his copper ear-pendants he broke it in half lengthwise and, seizing the child, cut off a piece of the umbilical cord with the sharp edge of the pendant. Another man rose and exclaimed: "I am his father!" and he tore off the child's right leg. Then all the men rose and cried: "We are all fathers of the child!" And they took hold of the infant's body and tore it to bits. Each man tore off a part and kept it for himself, until nothing was left.
>
> And ever since, each tribe, each group of men, has had its own narcotic vine.[14]

The story tells us neither about mutilation customs nor about any historical event, but speaks about the institutional importance of the *yaje* plant. The central Christian sacrament of Communion, the Lord's Supper, always involves retelling the account of how it had been established by Christ himself the night before he was crucified: "Jesus took bread, and blessed, and broke it, and gave it to the disciples and said, "Take, eat; this is my body.'"

Accounts of the beginning of the world, or cosmogonies, are the quintessential form of myth.[15] They place at the beginning what is "original" or fundamental in existence itself. Descriptions of the origin of the world represent the "first" of the series of forces, beings, and institutions that form life. Cosmogonies—which Westerners usually call "creation myths"—present a composite, embryonic picture of all the important and contending forces in the world. Often the actual physical origin of the earth is taken for granted, or at least given less attention than the origin of essential cultural institutions.

The different metaphors that depict the world's emergence—for example, God's will, cosmic struggle, sacrifice, and murder—are also clues to analyzing different worldviews. Some cosmogonies assume a primordial process of procreation, whereas others picture the world as created by fiat out of nothing. Some see the world as based on primal conflicts, whereas others see the "first time" as a primal order. Some picture the world as the body of the god, whereas others see it as "fashioned" by an ambiguous trickster figure. Some accounts are highly patriarchal; others feature an original union of male and female principles. In some models the world unravels from order to disorder; in others it progresses from chaos to harmony.

The difference between biblical and Hindu religious worlds is clearly reflected in their cosmogonies. In the Judeo-Christian account, every aspect of the world is created by a majestic decision of God. All existence is shown to be grounded in absolute, divine will and authority. But in the mythologies of monistic Hinduism, the original, supreme being literally *becomes* the world. It is not that the world is created by God, but that the world is actually an extension of God. It is a difference that underlies all other differences between the two religious traditions. One view is that the world is dualistic; it is seen in dual terms: there are two realities, the creator and the creation. The other view of the world is monistic, or in unitary terms: there is ultimately just one reality, the divine being variously named Brahman, Shiva, Vishnu, and so on.

Myths of the origin of humanity also reveal different values. Each anthropogeny represents the estate of human existence in its own characteristic way and gives a different version of the primal human fault. For example, the cause of mortality has been variously attributed to the first act of carelessness, laziness, lust, selfishness, stupidity, or aggression. For Christianity the original sin is disobedience, depicted as the cause of Adam and Eve's fall. For Buddhists the foundational defect is not disobedience but ignorance.

Buddhist versions of origins in fact represent a signifcantly different level of mythical thinking than found in most religious systems. Buddhism discarded Hindu cosmological myths and substituted its own schemas of how the samsaric world emerges as a function of individual ignorance and desire. The Buddhist "wheel of origination" depicts each step in the mental production of such a world. Buddhist myth is concerned therefore not with genealogies of social lineage but with genealogies of consciousness itself, and it gives accounts not of the origin of the natural and cultural universe but of the origin and end of self-imposed ignorance and suffering. Not all myth deals with the origin of cattle or clans.

The Immanence and Application of Myth

Myth has both a representational and an applied function. Consider now a few examples of the latter.

In religious systems, myth organizes both time and space, both the calendar and the map. "History" is organized around great, founding, mythic events. Jewish years number from the creation itself. Christians count time from Christ's incarnation. The Muslim calendar marks the year 1 not from Muhammad's birthday but from his "flight" (*hijra*) from Mecca to Medina—that is, from the first establishment of Islam as a community.

Myth not only projects ideal and transhistorical places (underworlds, heavens) but also creates sacred centers, landscapes, and objects in the visual world. Many tribal and traditional religions can point to places that mark the origin of the world. In Western piety the holy city of Jerusalem became the geographical center of world maps. Certainly every religion has sacred places where mythic reality is intensely concentrated. Sacred groves and mountains, shrines, churches, and temples embody the mythic world to the public eye; domestic god shelves and devotional nooks place it in the home. Visual representations of myth permeate the adherent's world through every conceivable medium. Healing masks, colossal monuments, body tattoos, the empty space of a Zen sitting room, and icons of the saints all keep mythic powers visible and real. Even secular nations have their necessary icons and shrines. Lenin's image is omnipresent in the Soviet Union, and the Lenin mausoleum with his embalmed body on display is a sacred pilgrimage site. The Lincoln Memorial has an analogous function for Americans.

Ritual is an equally direct demonstration of the immanence of myth. It is often a literal reenactment of myth. Christmas and Easter act out the major events of the Christian story. Every Jewish sabbath restores humans to the time of the creation, and every Passover recalls the original biblical exodus from Egypt—with each item on the seder table symbolizing some facet of the story. In Islam, every holy month of Ramadan represents the momentous time when the Qur'an "came down" to earth.

Every culture links critical passages in life with the dignity of mythic precedent or context. Navaho girls repeat the same first menstruation rite as set out by the primal Changing Woman herself. Every Buddhist layperson who goes on retreat repeats the "great departure" of Gautama. Traditional Russian Orthodox wedding couples wear crowns, representing the dignity of the first man and first woman prior to the fall. In other traditions the groom and bride represent heaven and earth.

Through ritual, humans participate in the very powers that ground their worlds, and the powers, in turn, are refracted in the stuff of the human condition. Consider the "great departure" rite. A Thai boy is expected to reenact the mythic journey of Prince Siddhartha Gautama—the Buddha to be—

away from his palace to the life of a holy person. The youth is obliged to "ride" to the monastery just as Siddhartha rode out into the night on his horse, Kanthaka. The horse's feet were supposed not to have touched the ground. The same must therefore apply to the boy's vehicle. An anthropologist reporting on the rite says that when a horse is not available, then "a bicycle, the back of a man, an open car, or even, as I observed on one occasion in Mae Sariang, a wheelchair borrowed from a local medical center might be substituted."[16] Here is the immanence of myth, the interplay of myth and human life, the weaving of myth with the variations of our local forms. The unconventional, makeshift wheelchair becomes Buddha's grand Kanthaka. Every Thai boy can be Prince Siddhartha. The mythic, archetypal power of the life of Buddha—or the life of Christ—is enacted again and again in the acts and lives of the followers.

There are numerous occasions where cosmogonies are recited during critical times in order to reconnect life with the pure forces of creation. For example, when a Polynesian princess becomes pregnant, genealogical chants are given to hula dancers, who then, while dancing, recite the songs continuously until the child is born. Eliade notes that this is

> as if assisting in the embryological development of the future chief by their recapitulation of the cosmogony, the history of the world, and the history of the tribe. The gestation of a chief is the occasion for a symbolic recreation of the world. The performance is both a remembrance and a ritual reactualization via song and dance of the essential mythical events which have occurred since the creation.[17]

Here is another example, from the agricultural domain, that Eliade cites:

> In Timor . . . when a rice field sprouts, someone who knows the mythical traditions concerning rice goes to the spot. He spends the night there in the plantation hut, reciting the legends that explain how man came to possess rice. The recitation of this origin myth compels the rice to come up as fine and thick and vigorous as it was when it first appeared at the beginning of time. He who recites or performs the origin myth is thereby steeped in the sacred,

creative atmosphere in which these miraculous events took place.[18]

Eliade also has shown how many healing ceremonies refer to myths of origin with the idea of restoring to the patient the original, creative power of life itself.

Mythic principles are recollected in times of need or crisis; healing, for example, in all its forms, is one of the central points of application of myth. Here, myth is the medicine for lost and broken souls and bodies. Shamans are skilled in retrieving lost or stolen souls from spirit landscapes, a feat that requires intimate knowledge of the spirits and their languages. Again, religious teachings are not limited to speculation about what happened "back then," but in their applied forms address immediate issues of well-being—questions of health, self-knowledge, harmonious living, evil. On the frontier of space for the first time, as their unearthly, marginal experience made them think of the world's foundations, American astronauts were prompted to recite the opening lines of Genesis. When Robert Oppenheimer witnessed the first atomic bomb test, the words that came to his mind were of the great god Krishna in the Bhagavad Gita: "I am become death, the shatterer of worlds; waiting that hour that ripens to their doom."[19] Many interpret world conflict and disasters in the light of scriptural prophecy—that is, in terms of a supreme mythic frame of reference that omnisciently anticipates all that history unfolds. The experiences of radical evil, disaster, or injustice typically force people to recall the ultimate moral or supernatural basis of the world.

In its normal, positive function, myth guides moral behavior, which thus "participates" in exemplary precedents. The Christian loves "because He first loved us," shows mercy because God showed mercy, suffers for the sake of the Kingdom of Heaven because thus did the Savior. One of the most popular books in Christian history is Thomas à Kempis's *Imitation of Christ.*

Because the study of religion in the past focused so much on texts and beliefs, the *practice* of religion, or what we might call "piety," has been a rather neglected subject matter. Yet the cutting edge of religious life is the application of myth to

the challenges life presents, both at group and individual levels. The forms of ingenuity used in explaining myth in order
to apply it to life situations need to be taken much more
seriously as a subject of comparative study.[20] And herein we
find the resourcefulness of myth. Much of myth's power and
endurance resides in its capacity to address and resolve conflicts
and contradictions in human experience. Sermons and religious counsel *apply* myth to the matters of everyday life.

Religious specialists are those skilled in the application of
myth. They are the shamans, diviners, priests, ministers, rab-
bis, ulama, gurus, writers of devotional tracts, interpreters,
and theologians. Every culture has them. They mediate myth
and society, exercising judgment in selecting from the resources of myth just those elements that are pertinent or applicable for a given occasion. Martin Luther King Jr.'s "I Have
a Dream" speech applied biblical categories to modern social
history.

Such specialists are an integral part of the history of religion. Many become exemplary within their own traditions
and contribute to their respective funds of oral or written
religious teachings. Through their lives and personalities they
add to (and conceivably, it must be said, detract from) the
myths of their cultures. The tales and parables of Hasidic, Sufi,
and Zen Buddhist masters show how richly and creatively a
tradition can be applied in the detailed settings and inter-
changes of life. A St. Francis, Honen, Gandhi, or Baal Shem
Tov—the religious virtuosi—can thus have enduring influence
of mythic scope.

The Transformations of Myth

Like nature, myth unfolds and realizes itself in various environments. It is seminal, alive, resourceful. It contracts and
expands. It reseeds itself and withers. It branches, recombines,
subdivides. It ignites. It shakes off its own excesses in times
of revolution and reformation. It appears in new revelations
to ripened times and to new *religiosi* disaffected by moribund
worlds. Myths have careers. The three largest world religions—Buddhism, Christianity, and Islam—were all transfor-

mations of the mythic worlds of their predecessors, and in turn they gave birth to countless denominations.

Myth represents a storehouse of images and archetypes that can be drawn on according to a community's needs and according to diverse "readings." Medieval Jewish and Christian exegesis recognized four levels at which scripture could be validly interpreted: the literal, allegorical, metaphorical or moral, and mystical.[21] Some rabbinic schools found the "real" text revealed through allegories based on the numerical permutations of the letters. The Southwest Indians have a common emergence myth, yet different tribes tell it with different emphases. The Navahos stress the elements of danger and strife; by contrast the Hopi think of the myth as a "charter for initiation into manhood"; for the Jicarilla Apache the story "becomes an unmistakeable allegory of gestation and birth."[22] The profoundly varied forms of Christianity find their justification in different passages within the same scripture. The Christian populace has found every conceivable significance and paradigm in Jesus Christ. Each age clothed him in its own ideals. In the first Christian centuries, the Redeemer is the otherworldly, cosmic messenger who leads humanity to a heavenly destiny; but in the modern period, Jesus became a model for loving behavior. The figure of Buddha, likewise, has proliferated into endless images. The largest Buddhist denomination, the Pure Land tradition, worships the infinite Amida Buddha as a cosmic savior whose spiritual merit is shareable with devotees, but this is far removed from the austere images of the more human Gautama found in early Buddhism, which sent the message of self-reliance. Some Buddha figures came to take female form, such as the popular Kuan Yin, whose role in East Asian popular religion is in some ways similar to that of the Virgin Mary's in Catholicism.

There is a certain paradox here. Myth—the eternal, fixed archetype—turns out to be creative. It reveals an internal elasticity, a capacity to unfold new contents, a play of applicability.

Myth is a central common denominator among religious systems. It is a transcultural category equally applicable to biblical, Asian, and tribal traditions, and it thereby serves as a fundamental means for building comparative perspective. Although myth has a similar function across religions, its content and style is different in each, and the variations and innovations in content display an astonishing history of world images and world building.

5

Ritual and Time

As myth expresses world foundations in terms of word and image, ritual dramatizes world foundations in terms of performance.[1] The two concepts, myth and ritual, are equally important in understanding religion. Indeed, the Roman term *religio* meant something very close to ritual observance. Worlds are formed not only through representations but also through actions, and a religious system is simultaneously a system of mythic language and a system of observances. Religion can be construed from either angle. We can study people through what they say, and we can study people through what they do. Time is a construct of ritual observance as much as it is a configuration of myth.

Ritual: The Concept

This chapter deals with the world-structuring and world-expressing nature of ritual. It focuses especially on the connection between ritual and time. How one lives in time is equivalent to how one lives in the world. Specially observed times, whether on a large or small scale, whether periodic or occasional, embody the sacred values of a religious system, while showcasing to the student of comparative religion exactly what it is that a given system takes as ultimate or foundational.

93

Westerners often belittle the concept of ritual. This is a result of an assortment of biases. From a rationalist perspective, ritual, like myth, appears archaic and subrational. Ritual is seen as a superstitious manipulation of magical forces, an attempt to ensure some desired state or avert some evil. This image of ritual as based on magic is found in many older comparative religion books, such as Frazer's *Golden Bough.* Ritual is pictured as acting out or mimicking forces that it thereby wishes to influence, as in pouring water to assure rain. Frazer called this "sympathetic magic." Festivals are also defined in magical terms—that is, as seasonal rites that attempt ritual control of the critical changes of the physical year.

From a Protestant perspective, ritual often connotes an inferior, superceded phase of religious history. As the ethical focus of postbiblical Judaism came to replace the temple cult of ancient Jerusalem, so Protestantism saw the return to the gospel of "salvation by faith alone" as surplanting the priestly, ritualistic system of Catholicism. For many Protestants, the term *rite* still conjures up not only pagan practices but also erroneous ideas of salvation by external works rather than by grace.

From the perspective of general public usage, ritual often means something mechanical and regimented. As one dictionary states, ritual is "behavior marked by prescribed rules."

As with other public stereotypes about myth, these culturally biased images of ritual confuse and impede the study of religion. As with myth, many interpreters have found the need to get beyond ethnocentric images of ritual to a deeper understanding of its unique structure, function, and language. Religious action cannot be merely subsumed under the notions of instrumental magic or sacerdotal regimentation.

The concepts of action and observance have a new centrality in the comparative study of religion. Previously, doctrine was the main focus. What was most important about a religion was its beliefs. But the emphasis is changing. It is now realized better how ritual and action are forms of expression in their own right. Whatever else it is, the sacred is something acted out.

One way to enter into an understanding of ritual is by seeing how varied its observances are in content. Some are large-scale, annual festivals lasting many days and involving total community participation. But others are simple and last only a second. The once-in-a-lifetime pilgrimage to Mecca is a religious observance, and so is grace before a meal or gesturing the sign of the cross. The Muslim month of fasting, Ramadan, is an observance, but so is the daily prayer. The Puritan sabbath and Dionysian orgy are both forms of ritual time. So are solemn funerals and joyous weddings. Ceremonial suicide is a ritual observance, and so is a fiesta. Feasting and fasting are both ritual practices. Some observances specialize in communion through sacramental objects; others center on acts of purification or atonement. Ritual time may be conducted by priests or professionals in a formal manner, or may have an open, festive, folk atmosphere. Monastic regimens ritualize every hour and activity in the day, but some laypeople limit participation to only once a year.

So observances can have any style and content. They express different kinds of occasions, acting out responses that are appropriate to the nature of the occasion. But what is involved in all these times, what all such observance has in common, is the factor of ritual behavior.

Ritual, in this generic sense, is the deliberate structuring of action and time to give focus, expression, and sacredness to what would otherwise be diffuse, unexpressed, or profane. Ritual is sacred action and time deliberately created. Like any behavior, ritual can degenerate into a mechanical act. But in its essential nature it is an act of concentrated display with regard to some particular purpose.

Religious life exists not only through myth but concurrently by a system of observances, some calendrical, some not. This chapter examines the variations on such ritual time in order to show the variety of ways worlds are expressed through structured observance. Before proceeding, though, we must describe more fully the two key elements that form the structure of ritual: (1) focusing, or framing, and (2) displaying.

Ritual as Focus and Frame

The basic feature of ritual is its power of focus. This focus can be applied to any content. The opposite of ritual time is unfocused time.

Ritual time is time devoted completely to a special purpose. Whether a tea ceremony or approaching the holy of
holies, whether a time of penance or a time of festive license,
ritual time is an occasion wholly dedicated to actualizing
its own purpose and momentousness. Ritual specializes
in the heightened, dilated awareness of the occasion it
observes.

Ritual time is the specialized instance of a distinction
taken for granted but operative in all experience—namely,
the difference between concentrative and nonconcentrative
time. Ritual builds its realms on the force of this distinction.
The mind can be inattentive, diluted, spread out; but it can
also attach itself to special projects with unalloyed attention
and acuteness of focus. In ritual, what is out of focus is brought
into focus. What is implicit is made explicit. All ritual behavior gains its basic effectiveness by virtue of such undivided,
intensified concentration and by bracketing off distraction and
interference.

A good example of ritual focus is the Japanese tea ceremony. The content of this practice is simply the preparation,
sharing, and drinking of tea. But it is the ritual focus that
makes it a ceremony. The entire procedure is performed with
a composed attitude. Every detailed act, every move and
position, embodies humility, restraint, and awareness. This
framing of ordinary action in order to reveal some deeper
significance—in this example the values are related to the Zen
Buddhist idea of the immanence of the absolute in the ordinary—is a common element of ritual behavior.

Ritual focus is not necessarily something subdued. Focus
can be indulgent. Take the example of the Shiite Muslim
passion play (*taziya*). Here is an event performed annually and
publicly as part of the festival honoring the martyrdom of
Husain—a seventh-century heir to the caliphate and a figure
whose sacrificial death has a central role in this system. It is
a time of high excitement. As the story is reenacted, audiences
at appropriate moments weep, laugh, and exult. Processionals
accompany the drama, with young men embodying the role
of martyrs by "flagellating themselves with chains and smearing
their faces and bodies with blood."[2] In the closing scenes,
Husain's decapitated head is the principal speaker and actor.

This is surely no tea ceremony, but it is certainly concentrated, ritual focus.

Ritual time constructs its own space. It is time that can be "entered" by participants. It is time that has an inside. Holy days are the best examples of this. The Jewish sabbaths have been called "cathedrals in time." Such times are like sanctuaries, with an interiority of their own. They are like circles one steps within; and within that arena everything incongruous has been kept away, and one participates in the internal time of the occasion. Like a picture whose borders accentuate the image while simultaneously marking off the impertinences and interferences of everything outside the border, such a frame at once enhances its own contents and sets off everything extraneous. In this sense, ritual time is analogous to ritual space. Notably, the Latin word for time, *tempus,* is related to the word for temple, *templum,* having in common the idea of "a space marked out."[3]

The spatial metaphor is amplified by the way that ritual times are often marked by thresholds. Because the time is nonordinary, one cannot simply move from ordinary time into the ritual frame without acknowledging the change. Outwardly, the shift may be signaled by the peal of bells or other calls to worship. Inwardly, entrance into sacred time requires a state of readiness, and the power of a ritual time is often in direct proportion to the amount and quality of such preparation for entering it. One gets ready weeks and months in advance for great, annual festivals.

Once within the potency of the ritual circle, time assumes a charged quality. Within the hothouse of its frame, the content of that time becomes real, alive, and effective. With the closing off of the outside world, the inner world of the ritual becomes resonant with its own life, its own momentousness, its own sense of the holy and eternal. Islamic tradition states that during the holy month of Ramadan the gates of heaven are open and the gates of hell closed, and that fasting then is thirty times more efficacious than at any other time. But the idea of a charged circle could be illustrated with more familiar examples. A newspaper article describing local American Thanksgiving observances reported, "Smokey's Truck Stop and Cafe in Kalama, Wash., offered free turkey dinners to everyone who said they couldn't afford it." Smokey's business had clearly been seized by and taken up into the non-utilitarian, sharing-oriented "time" of the festival and all it stands for.

Ritual as Display

The second general feature of ritual is that it is always a tangible form of expression. Always an action or performance of some kind, ritual is essentially a form of display. It demonstrates its point directly in the world of the senses. It is tactile, visible, audible, somatic. Above all, it is embodied. The language of ritual is action itself. Ritual does what words alone cannot.

Ritual can embody its truths in any kind of act. It makes its statements through kneeling, prostrating, sharing food, abstaining from food, standing, parading, washing, bathing, dancing, gift giving, decorating, dramatizing, inflicting pain, fighting, gaming, working, cooking, gesturing, chanting, remaining silent, dressing up, undressing. There is probably no human activity that has not been given a ritual value. And each type of act is an exact medium for expressing the purpose of the rite. Actions embody submission, sharing, obedience, celebration, purification, ecstasy. Buddhists have an observance of buying and releasing animals that had otherwise been condemned to be killed or caged. It is a ritual act of compassion. In a secular but altruistic vein, American entertainers arranged a "Hands Across America" dramatization for the cause of the impoverished. Again, the meaning is contained in the act itself. Ritual time always takes some natural medium of action and uses it expressively or symbolically. In all of these forms, humans are actors, not disembodied thinkers, and the truths of the rites are grounded in physical enactment.

The Protestants who thought they had banned ritual actually created new types of it. Protestant services just "frame and display" different sorts of Christian values than those featured in the Catholic Mass. Listening to Scripture, congregational responses, and even the more ecstatic forms of "possession by the Holy Spirit" in charismatic churches are all versions of ritual time.

To be sure, rituals usually include objects and settings as well as acts. Together these constitute the concrete language of display and dramatization. Obvious settings are sacred places such as altars, temples, and churches. Typical objects are icons, masks, and other images of sacred beings, and items used for purposes of sacrifice or offering. Sometimes materials for rites are gathered and constructed anew for each occasion.

Ritual sometimes has special symbolic objects that are used only during a particular ritual and not during any other time, thus enhancing the uniqueness of the occasion. These are objects such as Passover dishes and foods and Christmas ornaments and creches. Other cultures have the equivalents, such as a gilded begging bowl brought out just once a year at Buddhist Lent for a chosen layperson to make representative offerings to the village monks, or certain masks and sand paintings used by American Indians only on special occasions. All of these objects symbolize the distinct purpose of the ritual time. Certain prayers, mantras, songs, and incantations may also be used only for specific occasions. Christmas carols and the *Kol Nidre* of Yom Kippur are once-a-year expressions. Once-in-a-lifetime clothes are worn only at singular passages such as weddings.

Ritual creates an environment for the eye, literally constructing a visual universe. A cathedral declares the smallness of human stature within the divine majesty of the house of God. The open, imageless, and chairless interior of a mosque displays the equality, unity, and submission of the human congregation (the term *mosque* literally means "place of prostration"). The physical appearance of a Puritan or Quaker meetinghouse speaks out against presumptuousness and idolatry, against the idea that "externals" can mediate humans and God. An Eastern Orthodox church dramatizes the image of heavenly mystery and glory. And a Hindu temple shows the luxurious immanence of God within variegated, sensuous, outward manifestations. Even the simple sacred pipe of the Plains Indians is an image of the universe, with each part of it corresponding to some type of cosmic life.

Ritual weaves together acts and symbolic objects. Jumping over a fire may be part of an initiation ceremony separating a boy from his past. Wearing black and remaining secluded may be part of ritual mourning. Being sprinkled with water or a chicken's blood may be part of a purification rite. Placing one's foot on a stone conveys the symbolism of permanent fidelity in a Hindu marriage rite. Ritual everywhere is rooted in such physical, tangible symbolisms.

Ritual not only expresses; it also enacts. Ritual is instrumental in creating new forms of life and relationship, as we see in the vows and pronouncements recited at weddings, ordinations, and inaugurations. Ritual is authoritative. Its words and acts have the power of definitive events. Catholicism recognizes this in its doctrine that the seven divinely ordained sacraments are not just symbolic acts but actually channels of grace. In addition, ritual gains authority from the very fact that it is witnessed and solemnized before the collective eye. Seeing bestows reality, whether the event is a victory parade, the public execution of a heretic, or the installation of a chief.

We are now in a position to examine the two major kinds of ritual time and to see how it is that such time provides a key to understanding different religious systems. Ritual not only (1) regularly celebrates the enduring foundations of a world but also (2) deals with all critical occasions and passages. In addressing both the permanent and changing aspects of life, ritual ensures a perpetual grounding of time in sacredness at every turn. All of this is done through the varied "stuff" of culture and humanity, as the range of illustrations will show. We will deal first with the kind of time that is fixed and periodic, and then with occasions of passage and crisis.

Ritual Time: The Periodic Renewal of World Foundations

Every world has certain cyclical or periodic occasions of renewal. These go by names such as feasts, dances, holy days, rejoicings, resurrections, sabbaths, and campfires. Like places in time, they form a temporal geography. These points in the year are no incidental feature of religious worlds. There would be no worlds without them. Calendrical rites are not just a matter of seasonal symbolism. They are the points where a community renews and acts out what it holds most sacred, and these times are as central and definitive in world construction as myth.

Religious communities return periodically to what is most real and sacred because these become faded in the ordinary flow of days and weeks. On holy days the sacred gets restored. On what the Romans called *dies vacantes,* "vacant days" that were not devoted to a god and thus empty, the sacred was neglected, forgotten, or diffused, because of everyday human preoccupations. The periodicity of ritual time thus ensures the perpetual grounding of world in its myth. Through daily, weekly, monthly, or annual ritual time, myth is recoverable. Time, that in its usual course is spread so thin in quality, now returns to its source.

Ritual time often relives myth. The great acts that founded the religious world are reactualized. Every time the Catholic Mass is performed Christ's sacrifice for humanity reoccurs. In early Christianity every Sunday was considered "Resurrection Day." Every Christmas Day Christ is born again. Every Passover the Exodus is recalled. At relentlessly regular intervals— every day, week, or year—the "great thing" that life is based on, that happened in the mythic past, happens again.

The Annual "Great" Festival: Some Common Themes

Certain occasions function as the major, annual regeneration of the world. Standing for the whole year, they stand for the whole of time. Eliade notes that in several North American Indian languages the word for "cosmos" can also have the meaning of "year." Thus one group says "the world is passed" to mean "a year has gone by."[4] "Great" festivals are often connected with the beginning of a new season or calendar year. Such times have special richness and comprehensiveness, involving the entire community and every aspect of life in their regenerative power. To the student of religion, they display effectively the ideals of any given religious system. It is as if that system, that world, is created anew, in its perfect, pure form.

There are some important, common themes found in these major times. The most pervasive is wholesale renewal, total world purification. The typical annual festival has been called a paroxysm of world order, combining elements of extreme restriction and great excess, fasting and feasting, prayer and celebration, death and rebirth.[5] Homes and streets are cleaned, old objects (such as clothes and mats) burned, debts cleared, crimes pardoned, old images of gods flung into the river, scapegoats sent out to the wilderness, the dragons of pestilence and drought exorcised. At the same time, new fires are made, homes and streets are decorated, new images of gods are fashioned and installed. Thus the excess of Lenten abstinence is followed by the excess of Easter celebration. Muslims fast all day during the world-regenerating holy month of Ramadan, but every evening the fast ends and feasting begins. The great festivals contract the year back into their own regenerative forces. Time is drawn into the purifying process and the feasting. Much is expended, much is sacrificed to the pyre of renewal, yet the very excess of the festival releases energy and generates prosperity.

A major festival brings the totality of one's world into its domain. All ordinary activity is suspended so that the whole of life may become subject to the purposes of the occasion. For one time in the year, the entire culture is soaked with the force and presence of the sacred. During annual renewal rites the Balinese ritually traverse the island between the peripheral sea and the inland, sacred volcano, sanctifying the totality of their space. In one of their festivals a member of every animal species on the island—thus representing the totality of creation—is respectfully offered in sacrifice to the supreme god of Bali. We can see some of this totalizing process even in the festival of secular cultures. During the Soviet Union's annual Revolution Day celebration, businesses close and all manner of events—from the North Pole voyage of an atomic icebreaker to the successes of a milkmaid who yielded more than one thousand gallons from each cow—are dedicated to the anniversary of the "chief event of the century." Flags and banners change Moscow's color from gray to bright red, and even the KGB has marked the occasion with a string of white lights across its Lubyanka prison. The great festival is above all a public demonstration that the whole of life is under its aegis.[6]

Major festivals always reconstitute social relations and roles. They create a flow of communal energy. The festival provides for the group an experience of itself in its ideal social form, thus setting up paradigms of social existence that contrast with the imperfections of society during the ordinary time of the year. The festival brings out the "best" in people, however that may be defined from culture to culture.

If festivals reconnect what has become separate and regenerate social ties as they ought to be, it is typically done through gift exchange, visits among friends and relatives, feasting together, visits to ancestral grave sites, distribution of food to the poor, and general displays of compassion and good will. The Muslim Id al Fitr (festival of breaking fast), the main event of the year that immediately follows Ramadan and lasts three days, involves all of these elements. So does the Hindu Divali (a five-day "festival of lights" in the fall), the various East Asian New Year festivals, the Parsi New Year, and of course the Christmas season in the West. Major festivals such as these are characterized by full participation of all members of the community. During the Narragansett Indian powwow—their major festival—a circle for ritual activities is drawn, and all members of the tribe, including children, place themselves within it. The Parsi New Year includes a "hand-joining" rite, as do many Christmas Eve observances.

The great renewal time is one of particular exposure to the forces of destiny. It is a time of openness to the ultimate powers that encompass life. The annual renewal rite can include elements of judgment and fear, as well as elements of celebration. Between old and new years one is exposed to the governing forces not only in their benign but in their dangerous forms. The past is up for review, just as the new year faces new destinies. This is why there are so many observances at these times that involve divination, contract forming, repentance, and prayers and sacrifices for prosperity. It is a time of setting the course for the next cycle, and in traditional cultures this involves exposure to supernatural judgment. On the Celtic New Year's Eve, stones were placed in a fire and their positions the next morning showed the fate of the year. At the traditional Chinese New Year, the hearth god ascends to heaven to report on each person's behavior, a parallel in some ways to the figure of St. Nicholas who comes annually, reviews the behavior of children, and parcels out rewards. The holiest day of the Jewish year, Yom Kippur, is the day of atonement, a time of summing up one's life, a time of accountability before one's maker. According to the prayer book, the sins humans commit against God are forgiven, but for any sin against a fellow being, one must ask forgiveness from that person. On annual holy days, Burmese Buddhists honor their elders, saying, "If at any time I have wronged you, either in word or in deed, please forgive me."[7] The elders respond with their blessings for health and prosperity. Great festivals are occasions to make amends.

Annual pilgrimages are a variation on the format of major periodic renewal. The setting and symbolism is spatial. One must journey out "to" the sacred "from" one's ordinary existence. One goes out of a routine setting to a place of divine or mythic power—the gravesite of a patron saint, or a sacred river such as the Ganges. One goes from the profane periphery of existence to "the center." This is a different symbolic format than that of retreating to one's hearth and family (and closing the doors and windows). Judaism in biblical times required males to come up to the Jerusalem temple three times a year (Passover, Shavuot, Sukkot) for worship. For many tribes an annual pilgrimage to sacred sites is a necessary part of the year, since at those sites reside the mythic sources of one's existence. Pilgrimage continues to play a role in all historical religions. Many individuals perform annual retreats to either local religious centers or to international sites such as Jerusalem, Benares, or the Temple of the Tooth in Sri Lanka. For secularized people, even the act of going to a religious place once a year on Easter or Christmas can function as a significant "little" pilgrimage.

Annual Festivals and World Variations

In major festivals the sacred thing that is to be renewed is strongly highlighted, revealing more concretely than any doctrine just what it actually is that a community perceives its life to be based on. In great festivals life is presented just as it should be. Existence as it is most desired is set in motion. An ideal microcosm is posited and acted out. It is as though the ritual constructs a piece of theater that exactly expresses in subtle detail the actual, latent, and regenerative needs and values of a community.

A festival is a culturally intimate affair in that it is through the characteristic economy or media of a group that ritual time is expressed. The pastoralist Nuer of East Africa have an important annual event that involves ceremonially bathing their cattle—the primary source of their livelihood. Among the Eskimos we find an annual festival of the distribution of whale meat. The Ituri Pygmies have a yearly lighting ceremony for the forest spirit. On major holidays in the People's Republic of China, visits to public construction projects are often a feature of the day. And note that in this last case the sacred is not manifest in the economy of cattle, whale meat, or the forest, but in the terms of a socialist, industrial revolution.

The annual regeneration of values re-creates the very substance of a culture. Sometimes this is not merely figurative but literal. Because herders and planters depend on animals and plants for survival, their renewal rites express and assure this. Australian aborigines have annual Intichiuma ceremonies that regenerate a clan's own fertility and hence survival power. But city-states and nations renew the basis of their life, too. Since the authority and mana of the king was the source of good fortune for the ancient state, we find major rites taking the form of annual enthronement ceremonies for pharoahs and kings. In honor of its patroness Athena, Athens held periodic festivals displaying its own cultural achievements in the arts and military skills. In a great ceremony every year on behalf of the city, the Venetian doge "wedded" the Adriatic Sea—the basis of economic life—by ritually throwing a ring into the waters. Every modern nation has annual celebrations of its founding independence or revolution days. Historical religions renew their own spiritual "economies"—that is, the systems of moral values most precious to their faiths. The great renewal at modern Western Christmastime acts out paradigms of family togetherness, human reciprocity, and charity. The basis of existence celebrated here is not the Adriatic, not the pharoah, but goodwill.

Some societies find their ultimate security and standard in the prowess of males, and we are not surprised to find there a major public ceremony for young men's initiation. There are societies whose way of life is based on constant warfare with their neighbors and whose major festivals are constituted alternately by times of victory and times of mourning. For still other tribes the main event of the great festival is an elaborate food distribution ceremony consolidating mutual obligations, social status, and ally reciprocity. During this potent time New Guinea highlanders hold marriages, initiations, and memorial rites.

The annual festival magnifies the religious values of the society. Puritans observed no holy days but sabbaths, yet certain special, annual Sundays were dedicated to intensive times of summing up their lives. These involved fasting and repentence followed by services "renewing the Covenant." The two main annual occasions were a spring fast and a fall thanksgiving.[8] What calendar could better fit this lean religious faith? The week before New Year an American Zen group intensified its *zazen* (sitting) sessions each evening until the "first night."

Southeast Asian Buddhists have a major annual time that involves a fundamental category in their lives: the relationship between laity and monks. It is a three month period of purification known as Vassa, sometimes called the Buddhist Lent. Two of the three main festivals of the year begin and end this period. The season as a whole underscores the cultural fact that the monks are the embodiments of the sacred in those societies, so that to "renew the real world" is to regenerate the relationship with those who have wholly accepted the path of the Buddha. A highlight is the robe-offering ceremony, in which the laity, with great ritual protocol, bestow gifts on the monks. The climax of the event is the presentation to the monastery of a "great robe," which has been completed—from the process of spinning to the final stitching—in one day and night. Mythically, this commemorates the act of the Buddha's mother who made Gautama the first robe of his mendicancy in one night. The robe is a condensed symbol of the mutually beneficial relationship of monks and laity in these countries.

In traditional China the family system represented the moral and metaphoric foundation of the cosmos. The most important annual festival, New Year's time, reflected and renewed that system. At the holiest moment of the two-week period, New Year's Eve itself, families would gather at home, having sealed off the outer door of the house, and sit in a composed way in order of seniority before the images of their ancestors. Sacrifices and other rites honoring the ancestors were then performed.[9]

Religious sects and cults whose existence derives directly from a founder tend to hold major festivals that honor that individual. The original Black Muslim movement had only one holy day, Savior's Day, the birthday of their founder. The most important celebration of the Baha'i religion is the *Ridvan* festival, lasting twelve days and commemorating the prophet Baha'ullah's declaration to the world that he was the "promised" one awaited by all religions—a message believed to mark a new epoch of unity in the history of mankind. India has a Guru's Day, (*Gurupurnima*), in which the central role of the living master is celebrated, usually through *darshan* (appearances, or audiences). Tibetan Buddhist sects have important annual ceremonies honoring the enlightenment of the renowned lamas of their lineage. One such observance involves forty eight hours of uninterrupted chanting of the "guru mantra."

Annual festivals present especially good material for comparative study. They show common structures and functions, but great diversity of content, a diversity equivalent to that of culture itself.

Renewal: Days and Weeks

Renewal also takes place in the smaller daily and weekly cycles of time. The Muslim *salat* is a good example of small-scale renewal. Five times every day are set aside for ritual prayer: dawn, midday, afternoon, sunset, and evening. The practice shows that submission to God ("Muslim" means "one who submits") must be constant. The prayer can be offered anywhere, requiring no fixed location. It is always said facing in the direction of the holy shrine at Mecca, the God-ordained axis between earth and heaven.

Hindu *puja*, or worship, has a similar format whether performed daily in the home or annually at a temple. It involves honoring one's deity through the image in which the god is manifest. The image is accorded the honor of a royal guest. The attentions (*upacaras*) paid it begin in the morning when the god is awakened, and go through the day with the serving of meals, and end with putting the image to bed. The deity is often bathed, dressed, anointed, offered gifts, and even entertained. The overall result is a regularized point of daily focus for the expression of religious respect.

Just as with the year, so the day is a unit that can represent existence in microcosm. Everywhere we find practices of morning observances which in effect dedicate the whole day to a sacred purpose. Every day is in a sense the re-creation or rededication of self and world. Buddhist laypeople commonly begin the morning with a recitation of their commitment to the "five precepts" and make offerings before an image of Buddha.

The Jewish sabbath is the best example of weekly renewal. The Christian Sunday and Muslim Friday are directly borrowed from it. Sabbaths illustrate as well as any other institution the concept of the ritual framing of time. They evidently began in ancient times from the concept of a rest day, but the notion of the cessation of all work evolved into the idea of a time for the contemplation of things pertaining to God. Writing on the sanctity of time in Judaism, Abraham Heschel reflects,

> The Sabbaths are our great cathedrals; . . . Jewish ritual may be characterized as the art of significant forms in time, as *architecture of time.* . . . Six days a week we live under the tyranny of things of space; on the Sabbath we try to become attuned to *holiness in time.* It is a day on which we are called upon to share in what is eternal in time, to turn from the results of creation to the mystery of creation; from the world of creation to the creation of the world.[10]

The many variations on how the day of weekly renewal is observed demonstrate well the different religious values of Western faiths and individuals. For some the home itself functions as sacred matrix for the day, representing a kind of sanctuary from the world, while for others the sabbath is mainly a time of contact with church, synagogue, or mosque, and thus an expressly public demonstration of faith. Some observe the day with a strict sense of obligation, others in the spirit of relaxation. Orthodox Judaism observes the day in a prototypally "absolute" way by disallowing any traces of secular "work." New England Puritan public worship on the Lord's day involved spending both the morning and afternoon in church, prompting one historian to observe that "by granting six hours in the first day of every week for the clergy to rehearse the drama of sin and salvation before the people, New England put the Sabbath at the center of its temporal existence."[11]

Weekly religious time in the West is often focused at the service itself. For Catholics and Eastern Orthodox it is a time for the faithful to participate in the sacramental life of the divinely instituted church. For some Protestants it is the edifying time of hearing the preached Word of God, while for others it is highly emotional time energized by the felt, ecstatic presence of the Holy Spirit. The highlight of a church service is like a sacred time within a sacred time, and is always the occasion of some direct contact or communion with the sacred. In liturgical Christianity this is the holy moment of the Eucharist itself.

Traditional Theravadin Buddhists have the equivalent of sabbath days in their *uposatha* observances, the four holy days of the month that occur at the new and full moons and the eighth day following each. The laity may visit a monastery, give alms to monks, attend services that include repetition of the precepts, offerings to the Buddha image, recitation of holy texts, and sermons. The monks observe the time by assembling for mutual confession of any violations of the rules of conduct.

For some adherents, occasional renewals are not enough. Virtually all time must become sacred time. Monastic life illustrates the pursuit of the total sacralization of time. Every part of the day is brought into the framework of religious expression. On intensive retreats, laypersons can experience some of this sacred saturation of time. But the ultimate form of renewing time is that of devotees and mystics who aspire to experience every moment as the presence of the holy. This is seen in practices such as the Sufi *dhikr*—"remembering," that is, remembering God—and the Russian Orthodox "Jesus prayer," which involve continuously intoning the name of the deity. In this way not just every year and not just every day but every moment the world is at its source. The mystic aspires to live in a succession of such moments.

Other Calendrical Times

If the great festivals represent the totality of the year and aim at comprehensive regeneration, other anniversaries throughout the year specialize in important facets of world renewal. Most cultures observe not just one but many annual occasions, and these several anniversaries reflect that there are many significant realities within a world that require periodic acknowledgement. Thus in modern societies national, religious, and individual anniversaries are found side by side, and traditional folk festivals share the calendar with the major times of the historical traditions. Anniversaries of war experiences, of traumas, or of the beginning of one's commitment to a group such as Alcoholics Anonymous can be highly significant times. The totality of annual, fixed renewals forms a kind of calendrical map of the sacred for a given cultural or individual system, and the amount of energy devoted to a festival is a good indicator of its relative importance.

One common class of festival is that which acknowledges the spirits of ancestors. Some scholars have even proposed that regular observances honoring the dead were in fact the first form of religious ritual. Certainly the importance of departed spirits in traditional worlds is seen in the prevalence of these rites. In premodern China no less than three of the six major annual festivals were in honor of the deceased. The Bon festival in Japan, during which millions return to their ancestral villages to show respect for the departed, is still the second most important occasion of the year after New Year. The Roman rites of the *manes* and the Day of the Dead in Mexico became major festival times in their own right. "All Souls" festivals sometimes deal with resolving the status of those deceased who never received proper funeral rites. Fixed ritual times for honoring the dead also are observed at the domestic level. The elaborate, annual Indian *shraddha* rites, performed by the oldest married son in the family, are a good example, and many orthodox Hindus carry out rites for the dead daily and monthly (each morning of the new moon) as well as annually. Most religions include rites for the observance of death anniversaries. Even among modern nations fixed memorial days to honor the war dead and national martyrs are apparently universal.

A second, quite different example of a kind of time that is commonly built into the structure of the year is the so-called time of license. These occasions are socially acceptable or "legitimated" times that involve the suspension or reversal of ordinary rules of behavior. They may form a ritual time in their own right or be connected with a major festival. The premise is that absolute order 365 days a year is intolerable. It is part of the natural movement of time to deny this order periodically and set at liberty the forces repressed by it. In this inverse way, times of license have a relationship to what is foundational in society. Sometimes the time of chaos occurs exactly at the juncture between old and new years. Between the dissolution of the old world and the re-creation of the new, the old forms of life are obliterated. During in-between times such as this, existence is returning to its primal, pre-formal state.

The best large-scale contemporary example of suspended world order is Holi, the great spring festival widely observed in India during the last month of the traditional Indian calendar. Holi literally means "it is all over, it is past." At this one time in the year social roles and social order, so determinative of Hindu culture, are relinquished. Low castes are permitted ritual hostility to brahmans and landlords; prohibited food is eaten; erotic license is allowed; the power roles of husband and wife are reversed. No one is exempt from being dowsed with colored water, as if, for at least one moment in the year, all social structure and barriers are dissolved. For a time, all are equal. After the deluge, people bathe, put on their best clothes and go visiting. Even strangers embrace. Ill will is banished; the year is over.

Times of reversal are a common cross-cultural observance. During the annual Roman Saturnalia, slaves were served by masters and treated as equals. Babylonian customs made priests and kings the subject of temporary mockery once a year, and every year in medieval France a feast of fools was held (ordinarily around January 1, setting up a mock bishop, mocking church authority, and burlesquing the Mass. In the Christian calendar the world-regenerating time of Lent/Easter is preceded by pre-Lent festivals of Mardi Gras or carnival, during which "anything goes." Even Halloween, deriving from the old Celtic New Year's Eve, perpetuates in modern American calendars the archetypal time when the spirits are loose and children may seize the moment to assume identities and engage in behavior impermissable during the rest of the year.

Asocial forces therefore are given ritual existence. Licensed foolery and vulgarity, social reversal, and general pandemonium and strong feelings become concentrated in a contained festival time, thus allowing repressed unconscious forces to be given their fair due in a culturally tolerated way. Times of reversal fit well into the characterization of ritual time as that which makes the implicit explicit, and contravene the narrow idea that ritual observance is simply a measured, restrictive act.

Finally, we note the class of anniversaries that celebrate culture-specific skills, customs, memories, values, or achievements. One thinks of the running of the bulls in Pamplona, Spain; Hawaii's áloha festival; the Swiss shooting festival; the Orange Day of the Ulster Scots; and even Super Bowl Sunday in America. All offer insight into national character and worldview. On the birthday of Lenin, Soviet citizens contribute a day of unpaid, voluntary labor to the nation—a tradition going back to 1919, when a group of Moscow railroad workers voluntarily stayed on the job to finish work on engines needed to transport troops. Sometimes we witness attempts to fashion completely new calendars. Though not ultimately successful in replacing the old ecclesiastical set of holy days, the French Revolution's schema of a new, humanistic cycle of festivals showed clearly the values that the new order was to represent. The calendar included days to honor nature, the human race, the French people, freedom and equity, the martyrs of freedom, conjugal fidelity, unselfishness, childhood, youth, industry, and felicity. Today it is notable that all three of the major holidays in the People's Republic of China have socialist/nationalist content: May Day, National Day (October 1), and Spring Holiday (the old New Year).

Times of Ritual Passage

But ritual does not always take place at fixed calendrical times. Just as often it is a response to new occasions. Ritual deals not only with what is constant but also with changes and crises. It takes place not just when a calendar requires it but when events require it. It is a grounding force for critical points in the life cycle and for events that create changes in the order of things, and it integrates these into the mythic order.

The so-called rites of passage deal with great transitions in life—birth, adulthood, religious membership, marriage, death—but also any significant change in social status.[12] The new status requires ritual acknowledgment, and only ritual action can properly and fully effect the change. Through its demonstrativeness, ritual makes such changes real and gives them dignity. Through ritual, a person's status is transformed.

Each culture decides when an occasion is important enough to require ritual. Each will have its own weighting of the relative importance of different passages, depending on its value system and notions of identity. In some groups the funeral is the most important passage (Bali); in others, male initiation (the Masai), the wedding (modern America), or the induction of youths into temporary monkhood (Burma). Classical Hindu traditions acknowledge forty different stages of life to be marked with sacramental rites known as *samskaras,* or "purifications." These begin before conception (at various stages of pregnancy) and are completed with cremation. Among the Iatmul people of New Guinea, the first performance of any cultural act may be the occasion for a ceremony. For example,

> killing any of the following animals: birds, fish, eel, tortoise, flying fox; planting any of the following plants: yams, tobacco, taro, coconut, areca, betel, sago, sugar-cane; spotting an opossum in the bush; felling a sago palm, opening it and beating sago; using a spear-thrower; using a throwing stick to kill a bird; using a stone axe (or nowadays a steel knife or axe); sharpening a fish spear; cutting a paddle; making a canoe; making a digging stick; making a spear-thrower; incising patterns on a lime gourd; plaiting an arm band; making a shell girdle; beating a hand drum; beating a slit-gong; blowing a trumpet; playing a flute; beating the secret slit-gongs called *wagan;* travelling to another village and returning; acquiring shell valuables; buying an axe, knife, mirror, etc.; buying areca nut; killing a pig and standing a feast.[13]

Not long ago the most important major achievement of an Iatmul was homicide, and the most elaborate ceremonies, involving the greatest number of relatives, were for "the first time a boy kills an enemy or a foreigner or some bought victim."[14]

But the key moments of transition for becoming a monk do not include killing flying foxes or felling sago palms. Each system has its own categories of passage.

Without going into all the typical kinds of passage, we will concentrate on what passage rites teach us about worlds. Any rite, as we have seen, can be read as an expression of world. Consider here the pervasive, sacred role of cattle in the life cycle of an East African tribe:

> Cattle is the labor, the livelihood and the love of these people. A man's name is drawn from cattle, he is initiated into adulthood and elderhood through cattle, he marries by cattle, founds and feeds a family of his own with cattle. . . . When he dies, he is wrapped in a cow-hide and laid in a grave beneath his corral. But cattle—providing a diet of blood, milk and occasional meat—are not just the mainstay of life: they are the source of moral values and every emotion. It is with cattle that the god Akuj is approached, with cattle that the people mourn and celebrate. For the people of the Karimojong cluster cattle is the basis of their existence, a way of life.
>
> From childhood, each male has a special ox whose name he shares. He will make necklaces for it and sing it poetry. In battle, he cries its name. Should the beast die, he may even attempt suicide. Should the man die, his best friend will ritually spear the name-ox, for to let it live would leave a permanent distressing reminder of its owner's death.[15]

The role of cattle (= the basis of life) in one system may be filled in others by religious categories such as Scripture or Christ, which similarly ensconce one's life "from birth to death."

The things a child is invested with at birth, the gods or symbols it is introduced to, are the first indicators of how a community defines human identity and what it considers important. In Islamic countries, when a child is born and after

it has been cleaned, a male relative or religious guide pro-
nounces the call to prayer (*adhan*) in the baby's right ear and
the call to perform the prayer (*igama*) in the left.[16] The observance, at this first point of passage, reveals clearly the definitive centrality of prayer in Islamic life. In Christian infant
baptism the child is cleansed of original sin and thus made
ready for a life of grace, salvation, and church membership.
In some agrarian cultures the infant is laid on the earth, conceived as "the Mother of all living." Among the Gikuyu tribe
the small child, in order to become a full person, receives a
wristlet of goatskin symbolizing "the bond between the child
and the entire nation" and "linking the child with both the
living and the departed."[17] In the Soviet Union, in place of
Christian baptism, infants may be given (by robed officiants)
a "name star," symbolizing the October Revolution.

Rites of passage into adult membership, like annual renewal rites, have an especially overt way of revealing what is
sacred to the community. The purpose of the observance is
induction into the responsibilities of adult or religious life, as
distinguished from one's preinducted youthful or profane status. There will be as many kinds of induction rites as kinds
and levels of society. The focus may be on sexuality, economic
or survival skills, metaphysical knowledge, scriptures, or sacraments. Rites of passage are not always affairs of adolescence
socialization. There are also passages where an adult is transformed from a secular to a religious status, as in ordination
rites or rituals connected with joining a religious community,
or as in the internal, initiatory experiences that shamans
undergo.[18]

Adult rites often involve a set of specific initiatory motifs.
The radicalness of this structure is more important than in
birth rites because there is more old status to get rid of in order
to prepare for the new. The common ritual structure is that
of (1) some ritual "death" to the old status, (2) a transitional
period of preparation or "incubation," where identity between
the old and new states is in process of change, and (3) in-
corporation into the new status, with attendant acknowledgement by the group. With all its focusing power, ritual
makes effective the dismantling of the old status and its attachments, frames a period of change and testing, and incor-

porates the initiate into the new status. Often we find embryological symbolism here, an analogy to being in the womb of a new birth. The emergent identity might be marked by a new name, new clothes, or new rules of behavior.

It is just at this point that variations on the content of "new/old" become significant for an inquiry into worlds. What in fact are the different identities that people have been inducted "into," and how do these express the differences between sacred systems? Let us limit the examples to rites of adulthood.

Initiation rites that feature tests of physical skills and endurance are found in cultures where virility or physical, male skills are the supreme values and instruments of survival. But in imperial Rome a young man's most important achievement was to gain political rights. In the presence of family and friends he would put off his striped toga of childhood and put on for the first time the plain toga of manhood. He was escorted to the forum and thus public life, and his name was officially enrolled on the list of citizens.

A modern version of this political type of rite of passage is seen in the practices of some contemporary Marxist societies. East Germany was the first to establish socialist "confirmation" rites (the *Jugendweihe* ceremony) for teenagers, deliberately timing them to coincide with the traditional Lutheran Easter Confirmation season. Participation now is almost universal. On these occasions, the youths, after a period of instruction and field trips to national memorials—some include visits to Nazi concentration camp sites—take vows to work actively to realize "the humanistic ideals of socialism." The final ceremony involves families and friends, the presentation of gifts, and a celebratory atmosphere with everyone dressed in their finest. Soviets address adolescent passage in their "ceremonial presentation of the passport" (that is, the internal passport, marking full citizenship):

> There is an instruction period in the rights and duties of citizenship (in which pilgrimage-type "hikes to places of revolutionary, military and labour glory" take place). The ceremony is held either out of doors by a war memorial or other "sacred place" (*svyatynya*), or in a "Palace of Ceremonial Events," at regular intervals for groups (10–15) of

16-year-olds from the same district. Relatives and friends attend. The main common feature is an "Oath to the Motherland" read by one initiate, to which all intone "I swear!" The ceremony is most fully developed in the Ukraine, where it has such distinctive features as: (1) a preliminary minute's silence before an alcove in which burns a flame lit from the war cemetery's "eternal flame"; (2) signing of the text of the Oath to the Motherland by the initiates; (3) the roles of the State Mentor (a party or soviet official who conducts the ceremony) . . . and an Honoured Citizen (Hero of Labour, etc.) who exhorts the young people to emulate local heroes. The ceremony can be quite impressive.[19]

Religious systems have their own kinds of induction rites. Hindu youths of higher castes assume the "sacred thread" (symbolizing spiritual birth) in the *Upanayana* ceremony, signifying that they now assume full religious duties. They are ritually placed in tutelage to a guru, their spiritual father. They hear scripture recited for the first time. They learn the sacred prayer, the *gayatri,* that they will perform every morning for the rest of their lives. In Islam the major rite of male membership is connected with the circumcision rite (*khitan*)—often performed at a time when the boys have recited the Qur'an once through. If this takes place near puberty the youth becomes a full participant in Islamic ritual life.[20] Parallels are the Christian rites of receiving First Communion and confirmation and the Jewish practice of "ascending to the Torah" at bar mitzvah and bas mitzvah occasions. For some Protestant groups a "new life" in Christ is marked by a personal acceptance of Christ in the form of a conversion experience. Voluntary or "adult" baptism outwardly marks the new birth.

In Buddhism the sacred reality to be joined is not the words of the Qur'an or the spirit of Christ but the paradigmatic life of the Buddha. The principal rite of passage in Buddhist Burma is a young man's initiation (*shin-byu*), involving elaborate family participation and ultimately the boy's miniretreat in a monastery. The event has been traditionally considered more important than marriage or a funeral. "By far the most important of all Burmese Buddhist ceremonies," writes the anthropologist Melford Spiro, "no Burmese male is truly human—not to mention Buddhist—unless he has worn the yellow robe. Indeed, for the period in which he is in the robe, the boy—like the fully ordained monk—is not an ordinary human (*lu*); rather he is a 'Son of Buddha.' "[21] Much like a traditional American wedding, the ceremony involves printed invitations, costly dinners, and entertainment for assembled relatives and friends. The occasion represents as much an act of merit for the sponsors—usually the parents—as for the boy. In commemoration of Gautama's renunciation of his royal heritage, the youth is first dressed in princely clothes. His head is shaved and he is given a religious name that he will use on future visits to the monastery. He spends a period of time living the life of a novice in a monastery before returning home to regular life. Donning the yellow robe of Buddha is equivalent in interesting ways to the first reading from the Torah or the first Communion with Christ.

Sometimes passage has a more individualistic nature. Plains Indian custom required a youth to go off on his own— with rigorous fasting and prayer—to seek visions. In meeting his personal guardian spirit, he will develop an "ally" relation with a supernatural agency that will involve a kind of calling and will last a lifetime. Similar patterns are found throughout other shamanic cultures. Where life is ruled by relationships with spirits, the typical initiatory process involves direct contact with the spirit world through trance experiences and spiritual illness. Mystical sects from the times of the ancient "mystery religions" on have set forth stages of initiation not into the responsibilities and roles of society but into the inward, spiritual truths of the self. That modern people also may go through comparable initiatory ordeals and transformations of the ego, in the course of living through their own individuality or wholeness, is a point stressed by the psychologist C. G. Jung.[22]

Other Kinds of Ritual Time

The time for ritual cannot always be settled in advance, and it is not always connected with standard kinds of life cycle passages. Ritual time can arise out of any life situation. Critical and celebratory occasions have no calendrical predictability.

A crisis, an illness, or an offending state of impurity may prompt ritual action. Ritual time could be either a dramatized prayer for success in an undertaking—a healing, a hunt, a war—or it may represent a response to a perceived blessing, an act of gratitude for providence received. Captain John Smith noticed this type of rite when he described the Virginia Indians in 1612: "It could not bee perceived that they keepe any day as more holy then other; But only in some great distresse of want, feare of enimies, times of triumph and gathering together their fruits, the whole country of men women and children come togither to solemnities."[23]

Prayer is a response to certain critical times, and rites are often tantamount to dramatized prayer. They represent the same desires expressed in prayer, but through the medium of performances. Sacrifices, offerings, or rites of purification are nonverbal demonstrations of sincerity. Ritual objectifies and acts out desire, making it visible and explicit. Yet even prayer itself can be understood as a kind of oral ritual. The words of prayer are not just ordinary speech, but are intoned in a focused, sacred way, fitting the occasion. The relation of prayer to language is like the relation of ritual to behavior. Prayer, like ritual, is a mobilization of energy in the midst of chaos.

In some traditions, rites are pledged or vowed at times of special need. The *habisha* rite in India is carried out by middle-aged Hindu women with the overall goal of seeking from the gods a future that is delivered from the fate of widowhood. The rite is a "vowed observance" (*vrata*) and comprises a period of thirty-five days devoted to abstinences, continuous religious devotions for Krishna, and a special pilgrimage to the temple at Puri. An anthropologist reporting on the phenomenon noted that for the women he observed it had been a high point of their lives.[24]

Finally, Confucianism applied the idea of ritual conduct to the general realm of everyday behavior, thus showing yet another historical variation in the "content" of ritual focus. For Confucians, conduct in human relationships was determined by standards of ritual perfection. Their central virtue, *li*, means propriety, but also ritual, and in written Chinese the term is expressed by the image of a ritual vessel. *Li* stands for the way things should be done. As one sinologist observed,

"As used in early China, *li* would cover everything from the opening of the great doors of St. Peter's down to saying Bless you! when someone sneezes."[25] But most important, there is a proper way to relate to other people within every circumstance, so that rulers should "manifest" benevolence and subjects should "demonstrate" loyalty. The Confucian gentleman learned thousands of rules of observance—the proper way to greet a guest, to listen to a eulogy, to stand or sit depending on the presence of equals, juniors, or superiors—aiming at the cultivation of his character through harmonious observance of the ways of "heaven and earth." Ritual here is focused appropriateness to what *any* occasion requires.

A developed concept of ritual serves as an effective tool for understanding and comparing worlds. Defining ritual in terms not of magic but of sacred observance provides us an organizational category comparable in thematic power to that of myth. Ritual consciousness is not contained within our stereotypes of mechanical propitiation, vernal revelries, or mumbo-jumbo. Ritual profoundly shapes and expresses how we exist in time.

As communities inhabit different space, so too they inhabit different time. These times form an object of profitable comparative study. Ritual has a similar structure around the globe, but its content reflects different cultural and historical situations and reveals an enormous panorama of sacred and human values.

Ritual is not just archaic, prescientific language but a form of language in its own right, a form of expressive action. It "says" things that cannot be said as effectively in any other medium. It focuses, displays, enacts, creates, remembers, transforms.

Ritual time sanctifies the important moments in life. It defines the calendar and hence temporality. It governs—annually, daily, or whenever needed—the critical points of a world's concerns. It intersects ordinary time with enduring symbols and with alternating moments of purification and celebration, quietude and vigor.

6

Gods

GODS are a central, unavoidable subject matter for the study of religious life and require phenomenological analysis that is not governed by Western, theistic premises. Although gods are in some ways aspects of myth, they are also important enough structures in their own right to deserve special focus.

Gods as Religious Structures

We shall use the expression *gods* to represent a general *type* of religious experience. We will examine gods not for their intrinsic qualities as distinct, supernatural beings but as instances of a form of religious language and behavior. Gods are not just names and representations, not just literary, artistic or philosophic images, but the points at which humans relate to "the other." We adopt here not a traditional theological approach that assumes one god, "God"—with a capital G—to be the reality behind all worlds and religions, but rather a descriptive approach that examines how any god represents a way of structuring existence and hence amplifies our thematic understanding of religious beings and objects. We set aside unresolvable evaluative questions about whether gods exist

121

outside of human lives, and directly address how gods do in fact function in religious worlds.

The word *god* is used generically here to mean any superior being that humans religiously engage. Any being, visible or invisible, inhabiting past, present, or future, can function as a god. There are all kinds of such entities. For our thematic purposes, the category comprises a whole spectrum of mythic beings—more than what Westerners habitually associate with the term. Buddhas and bodhisattvas function as gods in many ways, even though they are a very different genre of being than the gods of theism. In traditional China the difference between ancestors and deities is sometimes hard to make. Kings, gurus, and other holy persons may be approached with the same behavior as that directed to divinity. The Greeks offered sacrifices to "heroes" and other demigods. Spirits and gods overlap in their functions and characteristics, and in Shintoist Japan everything has a *kami*—a term that, depending on the context, is translatable as soul, spirit, or deity. But there are *kami* of different powers and levels of importance.

Like myth and ritual, a god is a form of religion that can have any content. The content can be demonic or benign, male or female, limited or unlimited in power. It can represent the power of vengeance, kingship, love, ancestry, luck, territory, wisdom, fertility, consciousness, or being itself. A god can be endowed with specific character or personality—and given biographies—or simply representative of a force or function such as good fortune or cattle protection. Even within a tradition that has only one god, the images of that mythic being can be quite diverse. Phenomenologically, there have been many radically different experiences of the god of the biblical traditions, even though these are theologically understood as referring to one and the same god—namely, God.

Once again, in pursuing a comparative approach we must acknowledge the nets of semantic ambiguity. The term *god* means many things in modern Western culture, and understanding gods is easily impeded by any one of four thickly sedimented cultural predispositions.

First, it is not easy for a monotheistic culture to take an even-handed attitude toward gods when the very word *God* serves as the proper name of the Supreme Being of the universe, the one "before Whom there are no others." We have seen above how "gods" in the plural conjures up idols of tin and wood, the hapless competitors, so railed against in the Bible, of "the one true Lord." By definition, monotheism scorns polytheism and animism except occasionally to show that they are stages on the way to "pure" theism. In contrast to the observation of the Greek philosopher Thales that "the world is full of gods," the central creed of Islam begins, "There is no God but Allah," and the warning "You shall have no other gods before me" heads the list of the Ten Commandments.

A second bias comes from the side of rationalism, which typically takes all gods, including the biblical God, as fictions. Scientific explanation has done away with gods. Demystification of the universe is the goal of rationalism. Gods are merely projections of natural realities.

The third approach is the deistic, conceptualist one that accepts the general idea of a supreme being but takes it as an abstract, philosophical concept rather than as a religious presence. For many, the god of the West has been relegated to a principle—designating the ultimate force of order in the universe. God here is like a metaphysical hypothesis, to be either accepted as semantic currency or proved by argumentation. In this semantic context the word God often summons up a series of arguments for or against the existence of a supreme being. God is something to be argued about, not something to be sacrificed to.

The fourth bias is the universalist one that the main gods of the world religions are all versions of the same ineffable divine reality. Here Allah, God, Brahman, Buddha, and even Tao are but the various names for this transcendent mystery.

These approaches have their function within the world of their adherents, but tend to close off the process of observing and comparing what gods mean in people's lives. Rationalist and conceptualist frameworks see god language as on the same level with rational language, yet we have seen that religion does not share the same territory as science but is a different sort of language altogether. The discourse of science is disengaged, objective, and neutral to issues of the significance of human life or how one should behave. The language of gods—

as part of mythic expression—has to do with what acts one must take to lead a meaningful life. A world inhabited by gods is therefore not just a prescientific world but a completely different genre of worldview and world behavior. The two realms can certainly exist side by side, as they often do in modern culture, where the sheer differentness of their semantic form and context can provide for a degree of mutual autonomy.

As for the universalist view, there has been a definite value and truth to some of the parallels to which it has called attention. But insofar as it reduces gods to the same reality, it is engaging in metaphysical affirmations and transcends any real interest in comparative differences and hence specific worldviews.

The most important word in Western languages is the word *God*. Yet it is a term about which we have little reflexive or comparative awareness. It is typically insulated from inclusion in the cross-cultural subject matter of religious studies by its privileged place in living biblical language. In this chapter the god of monotheism is respectfully incorporated into a wider generic framework.

With these clarifications in mind we may proceed to examine further the idea of gods as experiential structures.

A god is not just a bare object—like a statue in a museum—but part of a bilateral relationship. A god is a god *of* someone or *to* someone. Only in the eyes of a religious person can a god be a god as such. A god is a category of social, interactive behavior, experienced in a way that is analogous to the experience of other selves. With gods one receives, gives, follows, loves, imitates, communes, negotiates, contests, entrusts. A god is a subject to us as objects and an object to us as subjects. We address it, or it can address us. Part of this relational quality is even evident in the etymology of the English term *god*, which traces back to a root that means either "to invoke" or "sacrificed to."[1]

The religious meaning of a god lies in what one does in the presence of the god. If gods are not just objects but constituted by forms of behavior between subjects, this relational universe sharply contrasts with the antiseptic, demystified world of scientific language where the earth is not a place of any exchange or engagement—where nothing is addressable.

In this absence of dialogue, scientific language flattens every-thing it sees into data, but in the language of gods, the world is experienced through categories of invocation, listening, and respect.

This dialogical factor may be understood better if we see how virtually any object can function as a "being." Anything can be spoken to. Poetry has always known this. And any form can confront us with its own power and message. An "it" can become "you" or "thou." It can be apprehended as "the one" that brings to us this or that effect. The evening news reported a falsely imprisoned man who found a turning point in his life when he met an object "he could talk to": a button. With the button he became friends and found solace. Religiously endowed objects easily become personified: the sabbath has been addressed as God's "bride"; Tibetan Buddhist shrines (*stupas*) are sometimes called "precious one" (*rim-poche*); the Sikh scripture is "the ultimate guru"; and the sacred fires of Zoroastrianism are addressed as though they were special beings. Any object, any "other" thing, can as-sume a temporary absoluteness in the way it faces and dominates us, in the way it forms a conduit between us and the infinite "wholly other," the "thou" that is the self's per-petual, complementary counterpart. Again, we both address and are addressed.

In the following sections we will examine two sets of variations related to the theme of gods. There are many others, but these are especially germane to our examination of the religious structuring of worlds. We will first see how kinds of gods correlate with kinds of worlds, and then look at the typical patterns that channel the interaction of gods and humans.

Gods and Worlds

Gods go with their worlds. It would be worth investigating the extent to which a god—in traditional geographies—could not really be worshipped outside its own land. In ancient semitic religion the term *baal*—"master" of a house, "owner" of a field, "husband"—meant the god who possessed some place or district. In the ancient world, priests were customarily not priests of gods in general, and not even of one god or goddess in general, but of a particular god at a particular site. The Bible tells of Syrian armies that, after being defeated in the hill country of Samaria, held nevertheless that the gods of the hills would have no power in the plains.[2] The god has its *polis*, its relative totality of influence. My great ancestors and heroes may not be yours. The territory of Ares is not the territory of Aphrodite. Nor does gentle Jesus the bambino rule over the same world as Christ the apocalyptic world judge. Protestants know nothing of the domain of the Blessed Virgin Mary.

Gods are not just fantasy symbols but beings whose realms cannot be violated with impunity. Where sacrilege does take place with no consequence, the gods have fled. We see this in the historical transition between religious worlds: when missionaries hewed down pagan oaks with no divine punishment, and when Polynesian taboos were neglected without repercussion, the pagan world orders with their ruling gods had already been abandoned. In a similar way, secular cultures have replaced impotent historical sacralities. Behavior that under the sanctions and surveillance of the gods would have been unthinkable in one generation is routine in the next.

Gods correlate with the critical points of a world where humans are most open to the power of "the other." If a world is crucially subject to what comes from the sky, from animal or plant life, from clan or political order, or from ritual purity, we may expect to find gods located in these junctures and conceived in these categories. In societies based firmly on family relationships and social hierarchy, such as traditional China, we are not surprised to find ancestors, elders, and emperors receiving the same reverence as gods. If a community or individual is weary of a despotic, alien world, we are not surprised to find gods appearing as messiahs, redeemers, and inner guides, delivering us to another, better place altogether.

Because the location of gods follows the location of the sacred, we get used to gods of mountains, rivers, vegetation, and fire; gods of the hearth, village, tribe, nation, and humanity; gods of thieves, merchants, smiths, hermits, priests, and mystics. There are gods such as the "One Great Source of the Date Clusters" (*Amaushumgalanna* of Uruk), and also

the "one great source of yogic power" (*Shiva*). There are gods
of the whole complexity of time (e.g., the ancient Iranian
cosmic god *Zurvan*), but also gods for collecting wood, gods
for cutting wood, and gods for burning wood. There are gods
of longevity, child protection, health, and success; there are
gods of death, misfortune, and every disease; and there are
gods who are called "The True Parent." There are gods who
are the sun itself and gods of the inner light. Gods are the
looming masks of the ultimate confrontational points of success
and disaster, life and death. The history of gods is linked with
the history of those points, with the succession of zones of
sacredness.

The connection of gods with irreducible areas of power is
seen well in the specialization of Roman gods. Agricultural
gods marked off the different moments in the growth of grain:

> *Seia* is the goddess of sowing, of the sprouting seed in the
> earth. *Segesta* is the shoots which have come up above
> ground, *Proserpina* forms the stalks. *Nodotus* forms the sec-
> tions of the stem; *Volutina* forms the protective sheath
> around the ear; and *Patelana* later removes it. *Lacturnus* and
> *Matuta* take care of the different ages of ripening, and *Flora*
> makes the plant blossom. [3]

The gods here are names given to particular life processes, and
of such naming there is apparently no end. We find that
"*Alemona* nourished the fetus, *Vagitanus* opened the child's
mouth at its first cry, *Levana* raised it from the ground, *Cunina*
protected the cradle, *Statanus* taught it to stand, *Fabulinus* to
speak."[4] Each part of the body had a god. Every virtue did.
There were gods of bees, sewers, mildew, broken bones, silence, and sneezing. Though the church fathers naturally rid-
iculed this specificity and taunted that in Rome there were
more gods than men, nevertheless as one historian of religion
wrote, "These were not sham gods, arising out of artificial
theories, [but] living . . . beings, who were worshipped."[5]

This extraordinary specificity of gods extended even to
powers of the moment. The Greeks "saw a special divine being,
a *daimon*, in each piece of fortune or misfortune. The trage-
dians speak repeatedly of *ton paronta daimona*, the god who
dominates someone at a particular moment, for instance during

mourning over a dead person or on being shamed."[6] Lightning and sheaves of grain were other instances of "momentary deities."

In traditional Roman Catholicism the polytheistic outlook was carried on to some degree in the veneration of a multitude of saints. Forty different saints were invoked in the French Vosges, as "guardians of livestock and protectors from all kinds of sickness, such as gout, toothache, and burns (St. Augustine, for instance, protected one from warts), as protectors in storms and against fleas."[7] In Asia we find a similar assimilation of native spirits to Buddhist saints. The name of invocation could change, but the domain (childbirth, smallpox) of the god or saint remained the same.

One class of supernatural beings is that of the negative gods: demons. Every world has its negating forces. The Satan figure in the West became elaborated as a diabolical antagonist to the biblical God. Minor demons, though, may be limited to specific functions, like drought, leprosy, or the weakness of hunters. The Ifugao of the Philippines count thirty-one gods who send dysentary and twenty-one who produce boils and abscesses.[8]

Some gods are patrons of specific communities of people. In traditional cultures every significant collectivity would have a sacred group spirit of some kind. Each of more than 400 Australian aboriginal tribes had its own, different totemic being—usually a certain species of animal or plant. Each village in Bali had its own barong, a patron protector in the form of a supernatural dragon mask. Latin American villages each have their special saint. In many societies domestic spirits or ancestors rule the household circle. The Japanese sun goddess, Amaterasu, is the ancestress of all the gods, the imperial family, and ultimately the Japanese people. Traditional Near Eastern city states each had their divinity: Melkarth was the god of Tyre, Moloch of Carthage, Astarte of Byblus, Marduk of Babylon, Jupiter of Rome, Yahweh of Jerusalem. Moreover, within a society certain classes of people were accountable to certain gods—such as warriors to Mars, seamen to Neptune, merchants to Mercury, and farmers to Ceres. Juno presided at marriages. In Greece youths identified with Apollo, maidens with Artemis, married women with Hera.

These examples should help us to see how complex are the domains and nature of the so-called supreme beings of the world religions. The supreme being is that god that grounds the entire world, not just some part of it. There are several versions of such unity—different families, as it were, of supreme gods. Many tribal systems refer to a creator god who is ultimately responsible for the world but has withdrawn from activity in it. In biblical traditions, theocratic images of power over the world—such as God as creator, king, and lord—are central. In Hindu tradition, ontological metaphors dominate; a common name for Brahman is "being, consciousness, joy" (*satchitananda*), and Shiva and Shakti are the "perpetual union of consciousness and energy"—that is, existence itself. Buddhas are defined in terms of primal, archetypal virtues such as wisdom and compassion. Chinese religion pictures the cosmos as the harmonious "Way" (Tao) of "heaven and earth."

For illustrative purposes consider the difference between Hindu and biblical images a little further. In the former, the supreme being is the indwelling reality of the world. In the latter, the world is under the monarchical power of the god, and there is an unbridgeable distance between the holiness of the Creator and the finitude of the creation. In the Hindu conception, all the countless gods are only the million faces of the one god. Krishna, as the supreme god in the *Bhagavad Gita* can say,

> I [am] the oblation and I the flame into which it is offered. I am the sire of the world, and this world's mother and grandsire: . . . I am the end of the path, the witness, the Lord, the sustainer: I am . . . the beginning, the friend and the refuge: I am the breaking-apart, and the storehouse of life's dissolution: I lie under the seen, of all creatures the seed that is changeless. I am the heat of the sun; and the heat of the fire am I also: Life eternal and death. I let loose the rain, or withhold it. . . . I am the cosmos revealed, and its germ that lies hidden.[9]

The biblical god Yahweh is more intrinsically connected with the symbolism of power, reflecting the kingship imagery so characteristic of the great gods of the ancient Near East. The Lord's "answer" to the suffering Job makes quite a different point than Krishna's:

> Where were you when I laid the foundation of the earth?
> Tell me, if you have understanding. . . . Have the gates of
> death been revealed to you, or have you seen the gates of
> deep darkness? . . . Do you know when the mountain goats
> bring forth? . . . Who has let the wild ass go free? . . . Do
> you give the horse his might? . . . Can you draw out Lev-
> iathan with a fishhook? . . . Will you play with him as with
> a bird? . . . Whatever is under the whole heaven is mine.[10]

Here the god is not establishing his identity with creation,
but his rule and mastery over it—the Hebrew word for God,
Elohim, has an etymological connotation of "power" or
"strong." There is nothing He cannot do: He made the world,
parted the Red Sea, and called forth his Son from the realm
of the dead.

Understanding the nature of the supreme being has been
the endeavor of philosophers and theologians East and West.
How are the many things of the world, including negativity
and opposition, related to this one principle? Why is there
evil if God is good?

But religion is not philosophy. Religiousness means engaging the sacred. It means having a focus, a point of engagement. These points are the earthly embodiments of the
gods: incarnations, authorities, priests, and a multitude of
symbolic objects.

The institution of the guru-disciple relationship illustrates
this idea of focus.[11] In Asian traditions the guru has some of
the functions of a god. The guru is a living embodiment of
the divine, a "realized being," a "living master." True progress
is possible only with the guidance of such a person, who initiates and prescribes one's spiritual path. To be in the presence
of the guru is to be in the presence of a god. The entire focus
of Christianity is on one great manifestation of the supreme
god—Jesus Christ, the Christian guru, so to speak. "I am the
way, and the truth, and the life," he enjoins, and "no one
comes to the Father, but by me."[12]

A god's presence can be experienced in virtually anything,
in shrines, words, and sacraments, in stones, and in people.
Hindu scriptures teach that the supreme being is to be seen
in all life. Sacramental religion finds the god in the rites of
church and shrine. Some ethically oriented Christian world-

views are guided by the words of Jesus: "I was hungry and you gave me food, I was thirsty and you gave me drink, I was a stranger and you welcomed me, I was naked and you clothed me, I was sick and you visited me, I was in prison and you came to me."[13] The religious person always knows *where* to find and honor the god, and with what actions.

Gods also appear within the self, as spirit allies or as indwelling elements of the supreme god. We have seen that shamanic cultures give importance to the individual's knowledge of personal supernatural entities. Many Christians testify to the presence of Christ within: "I have Jesus in my heart and I am no longer alone." Mahayana Buddhist traditions speak of everyone being "the Buddha." Islamic mysticism takes its cue from the Qur'anic phrase that Allah is closer to us than our very jugular vein.

Not all religious systems limit themselves to the idea that the supreme reality of the world is a being per se. Most noticeably in Asia, but also in some Western theologies and mysticisms, we find the notion of ultimate, divine reality as something utterly and intrinsically beyond any naming or representation. Hindu and Buddhist systems often point to an inexpressible unity of things that lies behind all human, subject-object distinctions. Said one Zen abbot, "There is Buddha for those who do not know who he is really, but there is no Buddha for those who know who he is really." The image of the empty circle in Zen symbolizes this state of having gone beyond the process of mental objectivizing. Buddhism is perhaps the religion that offers the most illustrations of the attempt to transcend gods and other objectifications in the pursuit of enlightenment.

Often we find two or more religious systems interwoven or side by side in one culture, such as an ethical tradition like Islam, Buddhism, or Christianity coexisting with an indigenous system of spirit observance. The realms of the *nats* in Burma, the *yang* in Indonesia, and the *jinn* in Arabia are examples of the latter. In Japan the buddhas cohabit the land with thousands of Shinto *kami*, the latter governing the forces of everyday life. Residents do not find these systems contradictory. In India by traditional count there are 330 million gods—and yet ultimately there is only one.

The religious significance of gods is not fathomed by just showing and comparing their respective realms. The spatial metaphor has its limits. We understand the life of a god even more fully when we examine the actual ways humans interact with it. The most intimately local ancestral spirit profoundly approached may reflect a richer religious phenomenology than a sublimely conceived being that has only a philosophical or literary existence. So we must now turn to the question of *how* gods are approached. If a god is a god only in relationship to a human, then how is this relationship enacted? How is a god's existence or presence acknowledged? Once again, we enter a world of variations.

Patterns in the Experience of the "Other"

Recall the principal: Gods appear to us reciprocally according to our attitudes toward them, and our attitudes toward them are reciprocal with the way gods appear to us. As the four-teenth-century mystic Meister Eckhart put it, the eye by which we see God is the same eye by which He sees us.

These patterns of interaction can be understood in terms of two main types. The first comprises those ways humans experience themselves on the receiving end of the relation; the second includes those ways humans are the active agent in the relation.

Receiving the Gods

Preeminently, a god is something received. This is connected with the sense of the numinous. Rudolf Otto's term is useful here for naming the feeling of being encountered by a powerful "other"—of being faced by a reality or being that is astonishingly greater than one's self. The contrast between this greater presence and one's ordinary reality is dramatic and produces awe, amazement, ecstasy. Otto and many historians of religion have taken this sense of the holy to be the source of religion, suggesting that doctrines and rites are but elaborations of numinous experience.

While the numinous is something that comes *to* us, it does come channeled through given cultural forms. Religious systems, by definition, anticipate the points at which interaction with things supernatural might or will occur. For some these points are visions and dreams, for others ritually induced states of possession, conversion experiences, church services, sacraments, faith healing, illnesses, contact with a holy person, divination, contact with nature, meditation, or private prayer. Many religions have begun with visions or voices. Moses is reported to have seen the majesty of Yahweh on Mt. Sinai, and the Hebrew prophets felt "the Word of the Lord" come upon them. The Christian apostles ecstatically experienced the appearance of the resurrected Christ. Islam is the direct result of the words of Allah that came to the nonliterate Muhammad via the Archangel Gabriel, words that were thereafter enshrined as the holy Qur'an. None of these experiences were solicited.

The experience of possession is common in many traditional cultures. Here a spirit, which may be either negative, positive, or something in between, takes over a body or personality. There are many societies for whom states of possession or trance are the regular religious avenues for contacting the supernatural.[14] The assumption is that humans cannot communicate with the gods in a merely ordinary mode of consciousness. But even in the modern West, faith-healing rallies continue to fill stages with the entranced, prostrate bodies of those who have been touched by the "spirit of God." Pentecostal and other charismatic groups make the direct experience of the Holy Spirit central to their faith. The power of their god is demonstrated to them regularly in such phenomena as "speaking in tongues" and spiritual healing. Worldwide we find practices aimed to demonstrate the direct power of spirit over matter—such as fire-walking or the handling of poisonous serpents.

Mystical experience, in contrast, is not a semiconscious or trance state but an intensely conscious state of union with or apprehension of the numinous. The experience itself is often felt as involuntary or spontaneous, as the grace of the god. Precisely because it is conscious, the effect of mystical experience is great on one's life and dramatically transforms, through its searing impress, one's normal system of priorities and attitudes. Many are the reports like those described extensively in William James's *Varieties of Religious Experience,* which speak of "that one great moment in my life spent in the presence of God."

For some the presence of the supernatural is received intensely in holy objects such as relics or icons. "Seeing" the divine image, or *darshan,* is central to Hindu worship. A Hindu goes to a temple, pilgrimage site, or holy person not for "worship" but "for *darshan.*" The deity or holy person "gives *darshan*" and the people "take *darshan.*"[15] Catholic and Orthodox Christianity focus on the presence of God in the rites of the Eucharist, in which the consecrated bread and wine are transformed into the body and blood of Christ. The bread and wine are not just symbols but divine presences. Moreover, any object associated with the divine can have the same effect as the presence of the god itself, and it is not surprising that "miraculous" cures are regularly claimed as issuing from contact with the humblest of these vehicles. Recently a thirteen-year-old boy was reported as having recovered from leukemia after the skullcap of the late Cardinal Cooke was placed on his stomach.

A broad, universally found form in which divinity is manifest is that of dispenser of fate. Humans find themselves on the receiving end of life. Gods allot destinies. They are often synonyms for fate itself. Relating to this "givenness" of the will of the god can even constitute a large part of daily religious life—as in the Dantean phrase, "In His will is our peace." Some terms for *god* actually mean "dispenser."[16] A true devotee is apt to "read" all events, negative or positive, as lessons in divine edification. The puritan Thomas Shepard thus wrote in his autobiography,

He is the God who took me up when my own mother died, who loved me, and when my stepmother cared not for me, and when lastly my father also died and forsook me, when I was young and little and could take no care for myself . . . He is the God that brought me out of Egypt, that profane and wicked town where I was born and bred, . . . He is the God that brought me, the least and most despised of my father's house, to the University of Cambridge and strangely made way for me there. . . . He

is the God that carried me into Essex from Cambridge and
gave me the most sweet society of so many godly
ministers, . . . [17]

Many will dedicate themselves to a religious life as a result of
feeling specially touched by some extraordinary event. In return for having his life spared during a terrible lightning storm,
the young Martin Luther vowed to pursue a monastic vocation.

As Job found, the Lord gives and the Lord takes away.
Gods dispense affliction, humiliation, chastisement, and destruction as well as blessing and mercy. The same puritan
quoted above lost his wife and son through a tempestuous sea
passage to America. His reading: divine instruction in humility. Certainly gods are not just expressions of solace for the
ego, and any theory of religion based on such a concept is just
neglecting the contrary evidence. Gods punish offenses, any
violation of their order. They bring down pride. Hinduism has
innumerable and terrifying representations of "the Destroyer,"
such as the devouring goddess Kali, pictured with necklaces
of skulls and bones. As a refrain, biblical monotheism speaks
of the judging, punishing, wrathful side of God.

Gods dispense, but also empower. They give power to
help against otherwise insuperable odds. Gods offer adherents
part of their own "life." Thus the great Buddha Amitabha
(Amida in Japan) aeons ago made a vow that he would not
enter nirvana himself until he had achieved such magnitude
of virtue and enlightenment that ordinary beings could share
in his liberation through sincerely calling on his name. This
invocation, the *nembutsu*, is the primary religious affirmation
of Japanese Pure Land Buddhist adherents, and consists precisely in the act of accepting a salvation that has already been
given or made accessible. This religious mode of acceptance
is an important strand of Christian tradition, too, as interpreted in the phrasing of a revivalist who preached, "In giving
you Christ, it is like God is giving you a one hundred dollar
bill: all *you* have to do is just accept it!" The affirmation that
salvation is not man's accomplishment but rather God's grace
is central to all major forms of Christianity. Hindu devotees
receive a new life when a guru bestows *shaktipad*—a touch on
the forehead.

Responses to Gods

Human responses to gods follow certain patterns. There are identifiable, thematic ways that people relate to numinous objects, and these actions form the stuff of much daily religious life. Two kinds of relationships are discernable here: the long-term relation to the god, and the set of short-term occasions where the superior being is enjoined in particular ways.

The long-term relationship is characterized by the theme of service and attitudes such as faith and trust. This is the realm of loyalty, steadfastness, and commitment.

One aspect of service is obedience or allegiance. Gods, after all, are "lords" of the world they embody. They have authority and in turn require fealty or loyalty. They are guarantors and maintainers of world and moral order. Authority is expressed positively in terms of obligations, and negatively in terms of interdictions and sanctions. Yet in the subject matter of religious allegiance we once again acknowledge cultural variations. There are different social forms of loyalty, and onto the idea of deity are projected the modes of allegiance familiar to the group's tradition. Traditional monotheism, reflecting the imagery of the king-subject relationship, made homage and obedience the primary themes of scriptures and worship, and made disloyalty to the god the greatest sin. An apostate was a traitor. There was a joint obligation here, as in feudalism: if the people serve obediently, the lord protects; if people uphold their world, their world will uphold them.

But serving a god is certainly not limited to simple obedience. The variations on service to gods are revealing and instructive. Gods are served in conformity with their nature, and followers seek to imitate or participate in the nature of their gods. One serves the god of wisdom through wisdom, the god of love through love, the god of compassion through compassion. The divinity who challenges false rulers, who liberates slaves, who cares for "the orphan, the widow, the poor, the outcaste," is a god served through social caring. At one point in the Bible, the Lord is satisfied by detailed kinds of animal sacrifices at the Jerusalem temple, but at another, when the religious world reflects the values of the prophets, we hear, "What doth the Lord require of thee, but to do justly, and to love mercy, and to walk humbly with thy God?"[18]

Thus there is some correlation between the nature of a god and the act of serving it. Demons have their followers. Where fanatic devotees of Kali the Devourer took it as their divine responsibility to murder on her behalf, adherents of the peaceful Tao aspire to be like the Tao. Where gods are departmental bureaucrats, the employees behave accordingly. What the gods *are* determines what it is that belongs to them, and what it is that humans have received and hence should give back.

There are also more specific, patterned ways that the behavioral relationship between humans and gods is acted out. By distinguishing and comparing these ways we get a sense of the spectrum of responses to deity that are religiously possible as well as a sense of the cross-cultural nature of the patterns. We identify here the following: (1) petition, (2) atonement or confession, (3) offering, (4) celebration, and (5) divination. These indicate that in relation to gods humans ask, purify, give, honor, and inquire.

The first type of behavior, petitionary, is that connected with prayer and propitiation. Humans need and desire things, and what they cannot obtain on their own they need to seek and receive from a higher, other power. In religious terms, success in life lies outside the control of the human ego and reason. People perceive themselves as dependent on higher powers, and acknowledge that their well-being is in the hands of those powers. Humans approach gods in order to receive critical guidance and support and to avoid negative or disastrous outcomes. To many an adherent, prayer is not an episodic formality but a sustaining way of life, and existence would be unlivable without it.

Asking things of gods does not necessarily take the form of simple petition. There are all kinds of ways to ask for something, and each religious system has its own protocol for what it takes to be effective propitiation, such as self-accusation, flattery, vows, conciliation, and meditation. Some words for prayer mean ask; others mean seek, long for, speak in a formal manner, or soften. Proper propitiation may take the aspect of formal rites, spontaneous personal prayer, or acts of asceticism. Different gods will have different expectations and standards for determining the adherent's sincerity.

Consider one example of propitiation from the realm of shamanism. Specialists in communicating with spirits while in trance, shamans are particularly adept in methods of direct negotiation. This usually involves a "journey." The shaman knows spirit geographies and languages intimately and is a master intermediary between his or her audiences and the spirits who control the affairs of the local universe. Our illustration concerns the descent of an Eskimo shaman to the abode of *Takanakapsaluk*, the mother of the sea beasts. This is done in time of illness or famine and is conducted in the format of a seance. In trance the shaman successfully overcomes a series of obstacles (such as crushing rocks and vicious beasts) believed to be preventing access to the goddess. Finally reaching her marine domain, the shaman finds a pool of sea animals. The report of this seance continues as follows:

> The goddess's hair hangs down over her face and she is dirty and slovenly; this is the effect of men's sins, which have almost made her ill. The shaman must approach her, take her by the shoulder, and comb her hair (for the goddess has no fingers with which to comb herself). . . . As he combs Takanakapsaluk's hair, the shaman tells her that men have no more seal. And the goddess answers in the spirit language: "The secret miscarriages of the women and breaches of taboo in eating boiled meat bar the way for the animals." The shaman now has to summon all his powers to appease her anger; finally she opens the pool and sets the animals free.[19]

The shaman "returns" to the seance, gasping for breath, and asks the audience for confession of their sins.

This points to a second pattern: atonement and purification. One must actively remove offense to the gods in order to avoid their judgment and be a recipient of their benefits. Petition is often accompanied by acts of purification. One needs to make up for something done wrong, make oneself worthy of that which is desired, rid oneself of any impurity that may be obstructing one's goals. Confession of sins is one format. Another is that of Chief Sitting Bull, who before an important battle would face the sun and make a hundred cuts in his arm. Prayer itself is often not just a form of communication but an act of humility, involving the chastening of self (or community) in order to be worthy of the god's gifts.

The third pattern is giving. One gives—just as one serves, asks, and atones—according to the nature of the god. Some offerings to gods are like tributes or even taxes, but while a material offering may be appropriate for continuing land rights, in return for salvation one offers one's entire allegiance and moral life.

There is reciprocity to giving, and Gerardus van der Leeuw saw perceptively that "the gift allows a stream to flow, which from the moment of the giving runs uninterruptedly from donor to recipient and from receiver to giver: 'the recipient is in the power of the giver.' "[20] The gift or offering sets in motion a cycle of giving. Giver and receiver are united in this binding quality of the offering. The more we give, the more the god gives; the more we have received, the more we must give back.

Sacrifices and offerings are the common external forms of giving. But to be effective they must always involve giving something that is one's own possession or part of one's own self. When an animal is sacrificed, it is not a wild animal but a domesticated one. In the bear sacrifice of the Ainu of Japan, the animal is reared among the villagers and treated as a member of the family before it is ultimately sent back to the gods. It is only a natural step in the logic of religious giving to shift from the sacrifice of foods and animals to the sacrifice of one's own self-possession, one's own ego. "My self belongs to God," say the mystics. The dynamics of sacrifice and its endless contexts and variations form an enormous part of the subject matter of religious life.

A fourth pattern of action is celebration, the human response to blessings received. This is the behavior of thanksgiving, worship, and praise, again as expressed in countless cultural styles. We have already seen in the analysis of festival times how celebration follows the nature of its objects and goals. The gods may be honored by formal composure but also by exuberant singing and dancing.

The fifth pattern of relating to the gods is through divination. The Latin term *divinatio* (from *divus*, "divine" or "of the gods") means the act of "reading" objects in the physical world to see how they express the activity or inclination of the gods. The premise of divination is that there is a syn-chronistic sympathy between the wholeness of life and each fragment of it, and, therefore, the action of gods can be de-ciphered by scrutinizing certain patterns in nature and inter-preting them as signs or adumbrations of the future. Augurs look to the sky for such premonitory signs. Others scan the livers of animals, consult the "fall" of objects such as sticks, dice, or coins, or analyze dreams. Divining is often connected with the need for auspicious timing. A leader might consult a diviner to determine the right day for a certain military venture; or a wedding day may be selected astrologically. The act of opening a scripture at random in order to find the divine "will" is a spontaneous application of the divinatory principle, as is, in a purely secular sense, the act of deciding what action to take by tossing a coin.

Gods are religious forms that have had every conceivable con-tent and scope, and endless local inflections. This experiential richness and diversity is often obscured by theological, con-ceptualist approaches that look at a god in terms of what it is ideally believed to be rather than in the phenomenological terms of how it is actually experienced. In seeing gods and their followers in experiential perspective, we emerge with another component of our framework for understanding and interpreting religious history.

Comparative perspective is not just a matter of judging the worth of gods, as in a beauty contest. It creates a broad cumulative outlook for appreciating any particular god or act connected with a god. It brings out both unity and difference in human experience.

There is no disparaging insinuation here that gods are mere inventions. In describing worlds, not only is the line between invention and discovery impossible to draw, but gods, whatever they may or may not be ultimately, present them-selves to human *experience* as "other" and as primordially given. Even from the point of view of invention, gods and their worlds would surely be among the astonishing creations and creative acts of our human species, and unavoidable sub-ject matter for any student of how humans choose to live.

7

Systems of Purity

RELIGIONS draw lines. They distinguish between what is compatible and what is incompatible with the sacred. In classical terminology, this is the separation of the sacred and the profane. More broadly conceived, the polarization of two kinds of behavior—such as pure and impure, right and wrong, appropriate and inappropriate, good and evil, holy and sinful—is a fundamental form of religious systems that has a thematic richness and structuring importance comparable to that of mythic prototypes, ritual time, and holy objects.

The phrase "systems of purity" will refer here to those many ways that religious systems deal with negativity. It will refer to the dynamic oppositions that make religious behavior a field of contesting forces and thus create the many versions of piety, integrity, and holiness in religious history.

This chapter explores a subject matter that is traditionally dealt with under such diverse rubrics as morality, good and evil, religious law, paths to salvation, and sin. There are numerous valid ways to organize all this, depending on whether one's purpose is anthropological, ethical, or theological.[1] But as with the other comparative categories explored above, we are approaching these topics not only in terms of the way they show generic, cross-cultural patterns but in terms of the way they illustrate and clarify the nature of world construction.

141

The concept of purity needs to be delivered from identification with particular Western stereotypes. It is not limited to such motifs as chastity or ritual preparations for worship. It is a structure of religious experience that, on the one hand, can have any content—different kinds of worlds define different kinds of impurity—and, on the other hand, shows certain patterns in the *way* negativity is handled.

Systems of Purity: The Concept

The concept of purity has undergone significant development within the modern history of comparative religion. Rationalist anthropologists in the time of Frazer typically assumed that early humans lived in a superstitious world of fearful taboos and were incapable of distinguishing the dangerous and the holy.[2] But recent anthropological analysis has taken a more egalitarian approach to the subject. Mary Douglas's work, for example, makes no invidious discrimination between primitive and modern systems of cultural order, but shows how any system will have its own version of pollution and danger.[3] Wherever there is an order of things there will be impurity, and wherever there is impurity an order of things is implicit. "Where there is dirt," writes Douglas, "there is system."[4] Pollution represents not just a mistaken fear about contagion or a prescientific idea about the physical world but an instance of something threateningly incongruous with or violative of one's world categories.

In its most generic dictionary sense, *pure* means "free from mixture or contact with that which weakens, impairs, or pollutes; containing no foreign or vitiating material." This is why the term is also applicable to soaps and motor oils, and why colloquial language refers to "pure nonsense," "he spoke pure French," and "the purity of her performance of Bach." Purity is a category that does not itself have any intrinsic meaning other than the state of being unmixed. Purity and its inversion, impurity, therefore refer to a form of behavior that can have any content. This is why they are a useful framework for comparative work.

Purity, then, need not be identified with the Western projections we place on it. It is a good term for the absence of negative or detracting elements within a system. It is a word that can increase our understanding of the religious structuring of worlds by connecting religious practices with concepts of integrity, differentiation, consistency, and unity. Every religious system makes a distinction between those actions that conform to its goals or subgoals and those that do not. Some conduct is fitting, and other conduct is not. Some behavior enhances the status of the sacred, and other behavior diminishes or contradicts it. Every system has its own moral compass. The lines, points, and polarities of that compass define the world of everyday piety.

Purity only exists in tension with its opposite. If the pure is the absence of the impure, the impure is the absence of the pure. The most feared profanities are often the inversion of the most cherished virtues. To those for whom authority is the supremely sacred thing, disloyalty and apostasy are the ultimate threats. To those for whom enlightenment is the supreme goal, ignorance is "the impurity greater than all impurities."[5] To those living a monastic life for whom chastity is the supreme gift to God, concupiscence is the direst seduction and sin. Whatever the religious goal, there will always be something to obstruct, oppose, or ruin it. The study of purity is necessarily also the study of its shadow side.

The differentiation of pure and impure applies to all levels of religious experience. Purity can be as important for the regimens of the body and for ritual behavior as for the mental disciplines of the soul. It applies to dietary observance but also to acts of self-renunciation and the sublimities of the quest for purity of heart. It can be impersonal or personal. The separation of right and wrong conduct can be rigidly and hierarchically imposed, and enforced by threat of supernatural punishment. It can also be freely chosen by individuals seeking the self-exacting, introspective rigors of spiritual callings and paths to perfection. The exorcism of profanity may feature spectacular, ritually exotic public demonstrations, or it may take place in the privacy of the despondent nights of individual psyches. The horror of pollution, the annihilation of what offends the gods, the fascination of the fire of purification—

these are inner as well as outer affairs, mystical as well as institutional acts.

The separation of realms is part of all natural, social behavior, as in the observed boundaries between adults and children, females and males, insiders and outsiders, superiors and subordinates, one caste and another. In traditional societies such distinctions tend to be inviolate, reflecting as they do the sacredness of a mythic world order. Social order is often the infrastructure of religious order. The elaborate dietary rules of orthodox Hinduism and Judaism are an example of the collaboration of ritual and collective identity, food representing here a coded statement about exclusive and inclusive membership.

Purity is the factor of consistency in every domain of existence. An Eskimo taboo that disallows a wife to knit while her husband is on a harpoon hunt shows that her crossing or tangling of threads and his need to keep the harpoon lines untangled cannot coexist. Their behavior needs to be symbolically consonant, not dissonant, with the goals at hand— that is, the successful harpoon throw. The symbolic world is here very much the real world.

In the Mosaic dietary laws, some species of animals are considered "abominations," but others are considered pure. Douglas has argued that the first kind of animals can be shown to include species that through some physical characteristic defy the natural order of divinely ordained animal classifications. To the Hebrew pastoralist, proper ungulate species were those that *both* chewed the cud *and* had cloven hooves. But the pig, rock badger, and hare, each have just *one* of these features. Because they lack the other, they do not conform to purity of type and therefore are unholy. In the water, likewise, finless creatures with legs also fail to conform to the natural prototype of the fish (a swimmer, not a walker). Such unclean animals stand for the mixing, confusing, or contradicting of what God has made discrete. Douglas notes that the perfect physical specimens in turn symbolized Israel's own need for purity as an uncompromised, consecrated community.[6] There is a connection here, too, with the myth of the creation of Israel: the Lord enjoins His people to make a distinction between clean and unclean *because* God Himself has separated the Israelites "from the peoples."[7]

To outsiders the detailed nature of religious regulations may seem trivial, if not inscrutable. But the microscopic character of rules is necessary precisely because of the complex, detailed nature of human experience. Every distinction—no matter how minute—addresses some real situation the adherent may confront or some symbolic unity to existence that the adherent desires. To the participant, purity rules represent consistency precisely *in* the midst of the specific circumstances and challenges that arise in everyday life. Thus, Islamic prescriptions for Ramadan fasting must necessarily take into account all the possible circumstances that make the practice valid or invalid, and the rules cover in detail every possible area of ambiguity. For example:

> It is not necessary for a person who wants to fast to pick his teeth before azan [the morning Call to Prayer—i.e., the point at which the day's fast begins] but if he knows that the food which remains between the teeth will go down during the day his fast becomes void, if he does not pick his teeth and swallows some of it. Further, as an obligatory caution, he must make up for that day even when it does not go down.[8]

There is a large principle at stake in such otherwise fastidious clauses: the deliberate, disciplined attitude of the individual. It is this attitude that makes the fast valid. Attention to the details of ingestion is simply part of the systematic application of the observance to the totality of conscious life.

Another area where the principle of incompatibility is a clear factor is that of contact with holy objects. The vocabulary of "sacred versus profane" originated in the context of the cult. Holy things cannot be holy, cannot exist, unless they are treated as holy. Where the presence of the sacred is powerfully condensed, as in the consecrated host in Christianity, the Plains Indian sun dance pole, temple altars, or even a guru, that object must be surrounded with requirements that regulate access to it and prevent its being compromised. Only the pure may approach the pure.

But what if the sacred is not an external thing? What if it is an internal state? The world religions all address the impurity of the human ego. In traditional Christianity each individual is born in a state of sin. Without God's grace we are sinners, just as in Theravada Buddhism the original human condition is one of profound ignorance and selfishness, badly in need of the Buddha's teaching. The individual then becomes the field of contest between holiness and profanity, and well laid out paths of piety and discipline define ways of bringing all thoughts and feelings into line with the religious goal.

Therefore, the opposition of pure/impure applies to quite different arenas of life. Where the sacred is located, there at that same point do we inevitably find the contestation of the profane.

We now focus on two ways of amplifying the concept of purity as a comparative category. We first compare some actual ideals of religious purity in Asian and Western traditions to bring more illustrative material into the picture and also to show how variations on the meaning of pure and impure take place even within a single tradition. Then we consider thematically the three typical ways that impurity can be handled. Purity is not just an abstract idea or a benign state of order. Most often it is something to be earned, something costly, something yielded through acts of abstinence, sacrifice, and consecration.

Variations East and West

The theme of purity has been elaborated in every conceivable way in Asian and Western religions. And just as important as the differences between traditions is the point that each religion itself will play out the many versions and possibilities of purity that exist within the horizon of its own premises. Each tradition has had extended debates over what is true piety and what is not, over what is permitted and what is not. Each has experienced schisms over such issues. Different models for holiness can therefore end up being embodied in

the denominations and sects that comprise the varied flow-
erings of an original root mythology.

Biblical religion is an instance of this. The "laws of
Moses"—613 of them, by rabbinic count—deal in great detail
with classifications of impure acts and objects, such as sacrificial items, edibles, body secretions, sexual activities, skin
diseases, and other physical defects. The laws also deal with
exact recipes for purification. These include acts such as bathing or sprinkling an "unblemished" bull's blood on the altar.
At the same time ethical interpretations of holiness emerged.
The prophets applied the idea of purity not just to burnt or
cereal offerings but to righteousness, justice, and "purity of
heart." And even within the legal tradition of priestly laws,
changes in interpretive focus took place. Where the earlier
levitical categories classified the intrinsic God-ordained impurity of specific objects and acts, the later rabbinical tradition
of the Mishnah classified purity and impurity more in terms
of what humans *do or intend to do with* various objects. The
mishnaic taxonomies of purity were more flexible and mobile
because objects with the same physical traits could be either
pure or impure depending on human attitudes toward
them.[9]

Jesus continued both the prophetic and rabbinic traditions, contrasting empty and external formal observances with
"true" internal righteousness. His criticisms of superficial outer
piety are well known: "Woe to you, scribes and Pharisees,
hypocrites! for you are like white-washed tombs, which outwardly appear beautiful, but within they are full of dead men's
bones and all uncleanness."[10] It is notable that a similar distinction is present in other religions—for example, in the
Buddhist *Dhammapada*: "What is the use of matted hair, O
fool, what of the raiment of goatskins? Thine inward nature
is full of wickedness; the outside thou makest clean."[11] The
point of Jesus that "there is nothing outside a man which by
going into him can defile him; but the things which come out
of a man are what defile him"[12] represents an idea about the
interior character of impurity that has parallels throughout the
history of religions.

The great mythic antithesis of human sin and divine holiness generated endless versions of Christian purity. St. Paul

faced the first-generation challenge of deciding whether Jewish practices—such as circumcision, dietary rules, and holy days—were necessary for Christian salvation. Conclusion: In the "new covenant" they were not. On a larger scale, the confrontation of Protestants and Catholics in the sixteenth century could also be called a contest over definitions of Christian holiness. To the Roman Catholic, the church was a divinely ordained institution for the dispensation of sacraments. But Protestants found the institutionalization of the holy all too profane and called for a return to the pure "Word of God" as addressed from Scripture directly to the individual soul. In Catholicism the saints were otherworldly exemplars of holiness and world renunciation, but the Reformers denied that celibacy and monastic life were any more godly in themselves than the state of marriage or worldly vocation. What was a medium of the sacred for the Catholic—papal authority, priests, altars, miraculous relics—was typically a profane affront to the Reformer; and what was holy iconoclasm for the Reformer was a desecration of the sacred to the Catholic. Protestants did not hesitate to rip out "magical" altars and destroy relic cults, and Catholics did not hesitate to torch the offenders as abominable violators of divine order and sacred authority. Each side interpreted the issue in terms of the holy/profane opposition. The Reformation was a confrontation over different paradigms of that polarity.

In the third and fourth centuries of the common era, world renunciation became popular as a Christian choice, and thousands left the cities for the deserts. Monks sought purity of heart through complete abandonment of "kinsfolk, country, honor, riches, delights of this world and all kinds of pleasures." They sacrificed their worldly lives for a higher vocation. They likened themselves to athletes striving for victory over the demonic forces of worldly attachments. The regimen was a rigorous, round-the-clock training program. Novices were taught causes and cures for the "principal faults" of gluttony, lust, covetousness, anger, dejection, boredom, vanity, and pride. They were enjoined to exercise systematic vigilance over themselves, discriminating every motivation, weighing every thought that passed through their hearts and minds. The soul had to monitor its own contested realm:

We should then constantly search all the inner chambers of our hearts, and trace out the footsteps of whatever enters into them with the closest investigations lest haply some beast . . . passing through has furtively left the dangerous marks of his track, which will show to others the way of access into the secret recesses of the heart, owing to a carelessness about our thoughts. And so daily and hourly turning up the ground of our heart with the gospel plough, i.e. the constant recollection of the Lord's cross, we shall manage to stamp out or extirpate from our hearts the lairs of noxious beasts and the lurking places of poisonous serpents. [13]

Whereas the monastic tradition emphasized renunciation as a way to perfection, the Puritans, in the Augustinian tradition, stressed man's utter helplessness at self-purification. [14] The Puritan was no spiritual "athlete" and no renouncer of the world. The Puritans' primary opposition was not soul versus world but rather God versus self. Subjectivity itself is here the very thing that is suspect. Man on his own has no capacity for purity. All he can do is expose his sinfulness and need for forgiveness so that God's mercy could be honored. The self *is* the profane, in relation to God. As one authority on puritanism writes,

Polonius states a humanist commonplace when he speaks of being true to oneself. Calvin sets out the Reformed position when he requires us to "rid our selves of all selfe-trust," and his words resound throughout Puritan literature. "Not what Selfe will, but what the Lord will," thundered Thomas Hooker. The self is "the great snare," "the false Christ," a spider's "webbe [spun] out of our bowels," the very "figure or type of Hell." To "lay downe God-self," to root out "the Devil's poison and venome or infection of Self," was at once "to kill the old Adam" in us, to defeat the infernal "rebels against the commone good, all [of them] private respects of men selves," and to strike a blow against, "Antichrist, that is, the SELFE in all." [15]

The Puritan searched out and exposed every tendency of the self towards its own justification. "Cunning" forms of "false holiness" were contrasted with God-given forms of "true holiness": the first fears sin "because it is self-condemning," while the latter fears sin because it "dishonours Christ."[16] Godliness and self-assurance were inversely related. The confident, spiritual battle (between soul and world) of the monk was replaced with the anxiety of the trap of subjectivity. Self had become suspicious of self.

Both monk and Puritan are what Max Weber's typology classifies as ascetics—of the "world-rejecting" and "inner-worldly" types respectively. Weber contrasts them as such with the category of "the mystic." Where the ascetic path to God is through rigor of conduct, through active struggle, the mystic's is through the cessation of human "work." The one follows self-reformation (e.g., purge yourself, be purged); the other, self-abandonment, as in the maxim, "Be still, then, and know that I am God."[17] So the mystic's confidence about the presence of God represents yet another type of Christian life.

A final example from the Christian tradition is the ideal of selfless caring for others. Mother Teresa of Calcutta, ministering to the sick and dying, is a modern embodiment of this type. Here is a different focus than that of the monk, the puritan, or the mystic, and here too is the imitation of a biblical prototype: "for I was hungry and you gave me food, I was thirsty and you gave me drink . . . " Purity in this form is not a state to be sought after, not a matter of self-perfection, renunciation, or inner enlightenment, but simple devotion to others amid an utter unconcern for self.

From the religions of Asia we select only a few examples from the endless permutations that the idea of purity has undergone. The Indian term for *Hinduism* (an outsider's word) is *dharma,* or "the eternal *dharma.*" *Dharma* is the moral order that upholds the world. To observe *dharma* is to act according to one's station in life. Every caste has its *dharma,* and there is even a term, *svadharma,* "one's own *dharma,*" applicable to a particular individual's life. At the same time, paradoxically, the path of liberating one's spirit from the world is also part of the order of things, and a renunciant's quite legitimate goal is to pursue a path of freedom from the constraints and oppositions of social and personal attachments. The *sannyasin* is the one who leaves behind worldly identity, including caste, occupation, and family, to concentrate on internal liberation (*moksha*).[18] At each point, what is *not* according to *dharma* is "the impure."

Buddhism, arising out of an early Hindu milieu, created an entire religious system based on a path of self-purification. Gods were not important categories in this new system. The standard manual for Buddhist meditation, *The Path of Purification* (*Visuddhimagga*), identifies purity with nirvana, the goal of the system, and the state of having rooted out all desirousness.[19] Desirousness rises from the predisposition to lust, greed, anger, and delusion. The central Eightfold Path methodically enumerates the exact areas of mind and action that require discrimination and perfection in order for the adherent to attain nirvana: knowledge, aspiration, speech, behavior, livelihood, effort, mindfulness, meditation. Probably no other religious tradition has analyzed so systematically the numerous varieties of mental impurity. In this Theravadin tradition, the monk himself is the living symbol of the path of purity. All laypersons are expected to observe the Five Precepts—the avoidance of taking life, speaking untruths, taking what is not given, unchastity, and intoxicating drink. Pious laity adopt additional precepts, such as not eating after noon, believing that through this they participate more fully in the holy path of the Buddha. Monks themselves observe 227 rules of purity, and these are recited in a fortnightly, confessional review ceremony to determine if there have been any violations— and if so, to call for confession and acts of penance.

In later Mahayana Buddhism, new ideals emerged. Mahayanists found the dualism of nirvana *versus* world to be itself a limited, ultimately "ignorant" fabrication. The real universe of Buddhahood knows no such dichotomies. All oppositions are limited human judgments imposed on a seamless reality. The state of true enlightenment transcends the dualisms that divide that which in the realm of Buddha nature is undivided.

Mahayanists acknowledge stages of enlightenment. Purity and impurity have a different character at each point of spiritual development. The path begins with distinguishing blocks of right and wrong behavior, with warnings about the dangers of worldly passions. As one's life becomes enlightened, the need for rules disappears. Further stages involve transcending the whole preoccupation with self and transcending the dichotomy of self and world. In retrospect, distinctions of purity and impurity were just temporary rafts toward a goal. The enormous pyramidal monument of Borobudur, in Java, encases these levels in hierarchic, ascending stone symbolism: pilgrims progress up terraces and stairways through nine different terraces, each symbolizing a station of Buddhist consciousness. The first levels depict mythic scenes demonstrating the simple oppositional contest of good and evil and are rectangular in shape; the top levels are circular and offer comprehensive views that transcend the dualistic concepts of the base. It is a striking visual statement—just as Dante's *Divine Comedy* is a striking literary statement—of how a system of purity becomes assimilated to an entire cosmology.

Zen Buddhism is a system of freedom through emptying. There is to be no attachment of any kind here—even to renunciation or monkhood. The very figure of Buddha, insofar as it becomes an *object,* is an illusion. Some Zen monasteries put scriptures in their toilet rooms to demonstrate that truth is not a matter of words. Pictures of Bodhidharma, the patriarch who brought Zen to China, show him scowling absurdly at anyone foolish enough to look "objectively" at the picture— and thus away from themselves—for enlightenment. The great symbol of truth in Zen is the empty circle, signifying the absence of illusions of every kind.

Purity in Buddhism is focused on consciousness itself. One does not become a Buddhist saint merely by matted hair, lineage or caste. The liberated one is the person who has broken the bonds not only of world attachment but of all internal self-delusion. Purity is assimilated not with cleanness or order but with inner freedom, often summed up in such symbols as nirvana or nothingness (*sunyata*).

Ways of Dealing with Impurity

We are now in a position to review the types of ways impurity can be handled. There is no limit to the techniques and styles by which religious people deal with threats and dissonance, but there are three typical patterns that stand out, each admitting of numerous subvariations. These ways are: (1) avoidance of profanity, (2) purification of profanity, and (3) transcending the opposition of profanity/purity. A religious system preserves the sacred by differentiating itself from all

that is incompatible with it; or it purges impurity that has not
been kept apart but has somehow become part of one's system;
or it overcomes or integrates oppositions from a "higher" point
of view. We keep the enemy at bay, demolish it, or cease to
treat it as an enemy at all, depending on pivoting contexts.
We avoid guilt; we are guilty; we are accepted or forgiven.
These are the patterns that in one way or other govern the
daily religious life of most people.

Avoidance

Profanity is first of all something to be avoided. It is natural
that much religious behavior is defensive or preventive. Pres-
ervation of territory is a strong instinct. The sacred thing is
here the circumscribed, safeguarded, inviolable thing. Religions keep trouble out by declaring specific actions to be out
of bounds, by carefully delineating proper and improper conduct. Religious laws often tell adherents what *not* to do, as in
the Ten Commandments of the Bible and the Five Precepts
of Buddhism.

Avoidance behavior can take numerous forms through
varieties of prohibition, detachment, and abstention. Examples of this go well beyond Eskimo knitting taboos. Consider
the Hindu idea of karma yoga as set forth in the Bhagavad
Gita. Here the god Krishna teaches the warrior Arjuna to act
in the arena of his legitimate duties, but to abandon all attachment to the results of his actions. By offering all his actions, dutifully performed, to Krishna, and disidentifying with
them personally, Arjuna will remain unsoiled and unimpris-
oned by the profanity that comes with identifying his self with
his conduct. As "the lotus leaf rests unwetted by water," so
the enlightened person "rests on action, untouched by
action."[20]

Sometimes controlled behavior is reinforced by threats of
supernatural punishment and by mythologizing the evil of the
thing to be avoided. Hellfire can be inhibiting. Impurity labeled satanic is doubly to be repudiated.

History in general and religious history in particular show
us the many things humans will do in order to avoid pollution,
shame, or dishonor. The martyr will gladly give up life itself
rather than tolerate profanation of the holy. Monasteries built

isolated realms on the tops of inaccessible mountains. Quakers refused to doff their hats to any human. Religious schools still attempt to protect children from contact with secular theories and mores. The subject matter here: worlds shut out, profanity shunned, bulwarks erected, lines not crossed, refusals to follow "man's law, instead of God law." The results: existence unified, the sacred kept intact, integrity maintained.

Purification

Keeping away profanity is one thing, but dealing with it after it is present is quite another. Impurity that has *already* contaminated sacred order is intolerable and must be ridded by some means appropriate to the nature of the violation. The forms this takes make up a huge and diverse religious phenomenology. At one extreme is the gentle practice of the Tenri Kyo religion of Japan: impure "dust" is "swept" away in rhythmic, ritual gestures of the hands and arms. At the other extreme are public tortures and executions, demonstrating that the horror and absoluteness of the crime—that is, an act of sacrilege that defies the foundations of the world—requires a commensurate horror and absoluteness of destruction. Some offenses to the cosmos are unmitigated evil, to be expunged absolutely, while other infractions require only an apology. Depending on the seriousness and kind of the pollution, communities purify profanation in different ways: punishment, banishment, shunning, use of scapegoats, exorcism, ritual combat, excommunication, required penance, imprisonment, pronounced forgiveness or pardon, rehabilitation. Profanity is destroyed, expunged, condemned, chastened, relinquished, abandoned, locked up. These are inflicted on the guilty person by the system. From the point of view of the individual as agent of self-purification, we find acts of repentance, atonement, expiation, discipline, confession, isolation, fasting, apology, "soul-searching," and prayer. Sometimes purification is effected with material means, such as water, fire, smoke, urine, emetics, cow dung, sun, rain, steam baths, ice baths, ashes, mud, noise, oil, green branches, or blood. The psychology of purgation will vary with mythic contexts and native categories.

Sacrifice is one of the most universal forms of religious behavior and a prominent example of purification. Some consider it the religious category par excellence, the supreme religious act. To sacrifice, literally, is to make sacred. It is the sacrificer that is consecrated, made sacred or pure, by the act of giving up possession. The thing sacrificed must always be of value. The subject matter of sacrifice takes us from the simple throw of a coin—an offering—to the heroics of self-immolation or religious suicide; from offering chickens and oxen in order to satisfy the local gods, to the mystical relinquishing of selfhood itself. Sacrifice can be a long, slow process or a sudden paroxysm. It can be active or passive—that is, "through the soul's efforts or through God's grace." It is not only riddance, but also preparation to receive.

The sacrifice of self is an important theme in the lives of saints and mystics. The self—meaning one's ordinary ego system—is here the consecrated victim, the substance offered to the fire. Illnesses that are tantamount to a death qualify a shaman to become a healer. The one who has become "like a corpse" and returns, the one who has in one way or another relinquished hold on one's life, is the one in whom the regenerative, supernatural forces of life and healing can be activated. Accounts of initiatory illnesses of shamans—in which they experience themselves as completely dismembered—run parallel to the mortifications of a Christian such as St. Teresa of Avila, who lay in cold paralysis for three years and had several times been pronounced dead, before being given her new life "from God." Profound ascetic self-renunciation, in Hindu and Buddhist tradition, creates a sanctity that puts the saint on a higher level than the gods, a sanctity "that makes the gods tremble."

Some religions understand various kinds of sufferings to be God's means of purifying the soul. As examples, one Catholic theologian cites "war, persecution, calumny, imprisonment, injustice, abuse of authority, sickness, accident, poverty, failure, scandal, ingratitude, the loss of loved ones, conflict and misunderstanding arising from differences of opinion and temperament, and even the suffering of death." The writer goes on to say that the steady fulfillment of daily duties, according to one's state in life, "demands heroic virtue, and the burden of these duties may well serve as an instrument of purification."[21]

Transcending the Purity/Profanity Opposition

There is another possible way of relating to profanity besides avoiding it and purifying it, and that is to overcome the ordinary dichotomy of purity and profanity. Within many religions we find the idea that pure and impure are ultimately man-made and that there is a higher perspective on the world—a higher purity, as it were—that involves the acceptance of opposites. The real world—for example, the world of Buddha or the world of God—is seen as a unity. St. Paul preached the Christian life as a "new creation" that transcended the distinctions of Greek or Jew, circumcised or uncircumcised, slave or free, male or female, and that transcended any outer requirements of works or ritual observance. "There is nothing unclean of itself," St. Paul advised; and another New Testament writer adds, "To the pure all things are pure."[22]

Wherever the world has been divided into spirit and matter, God and nature, soul and body, higher and lower, clean and unclean, superior and inferior social rank—there, too, in the dialectics of religious thinking, we find attempts to overcome what has been so split. So while there are those religious regimens based on disengaging pure and impure realms, others put more emphasis on dealing *with* the impure (or worldly, or chaotic) realm and transforming it.

Some religions maintain a ritual respect for both the beneficent and demonic forces that rule their world. The impure can be construed as an extraordinary, transhuman force. A regularly performed Balinese ritual drama represents two supernatural forces—the positive one represented as a dragon and the negative one as a witch—engaged in a kind of perpetual complementarity of power. Yoruba communal rites have a sacramental dish on which is pictured Eshu, the primary trickster figure of their universe, as if to not neglect the "left hand" of God, and as if to say that Eshu must exist in order to let the supreme god (Ifa or Orunmila) defeat him. The first portion of sacrifices to the gods are set apart for Eshu, to ensure his mediating influence. Among the African Lele, the most

sacred and heavily tabooed object, the pangolin or scaly ant-
eater, is occasionally eaten in a solemn ceremonial. Douglas
cites the act as representing a kind of hidden cosmic unity of
life and death that overrides the conventional lines of purity.[23]
Many are the instances where profane objects and acts get
invested with supernatural and even sacred value precisely
because they stand out from ordinary objects and acts and thus
seem to be part of another world of power.

The reunification of sacred and profane is observable in
practices of *accepting* the unclean or rejected side of a polarity
in the name of a higher, mediating spiritual reality. In worlds
where social hierarchy has become invidious and despotic, we
find a Jesus associating with "impure" tax collectors and a
Gandhi embracing outcastes. Social boundaries become an
occasion for their own religious dismantling and for affirming
the immanence of the holy. Certain forms of meditative practice such as "left-handed" tantric yoga make it a point to
participate in normally "unclean" kinds of behavior—such as
eating meat, drinking wine, and sexual intercourse—in order
to manifest the principle of the secret unitary nature of the
world. The ideal of a liberated soul so free, holy, and invul-
nerable to profanity that it can live in the midst of "unclean"
worldliness and not be violated by it, is an ideal found in both
Asian and Western religious traditions. "When he has no lust,
no hatred," says the Bhagavad Gita, "a man walks safely among
the things of lust and hatred."[24] In Jesus' Sermon on the
Mount, the injunction to "turn the other cheek" implies having a self pure enough to accept offense and mockery without
resorting to profanity of its own.

Where profanity and offense are overcome within, then
they are already overcome without. If the mind is clear and
pure, then the hands cannot be defiled. A Zen story illustrates
this.

> Tanzan and Ekido were once traveling together down a
> muddy road. A heavy rain was still falling.
>   Coming around a bend, they met a lovely girl in a silk
> kimono and sash, unable to cross the intersection.
>   "Come on, girl," said Tanzan at once. Lifting her in
> his arms, he carried her over the mud.
>   Ekido did not speak again until that night when they

reached a lodging temple. Then he no longer could restrain himself. "We monks don't go near females," he told Tanzan, "especially not young and lovely ones. It is dangerous. Why did you do that?"

"I left the girl there," said Tanzan. "Are you still carrying her?"[25]

To Tanzan the girl as such is not impure, only the thought of desire for her. Tanzan remained unprofaned by the event. The point: for those still struggling with the world and with the pure/impure contest inside themselves, the outside world continues to mirror these distinctions.

The Relativity of Purity within a System

Within a religious culture the sacred/profane polarity is not monolithic but complex. It is relative to social and religious location. It is positional, relational. The anthropologist Arnold van Gennep writes of this notion of "the pivoting of the sacred" as follows:

> Characteristically, the presence of the sacred . . . is variable. Sacredness as an attribute is not absolute; it is brought into play by the nature of particular situations. A man at home, in his tribe, lives in the secular realm; he moves into the realm of the sacred when he goes on a journey and finds himself a foreigner near a camp of strangers. A Brahman belongs to the sacred world by birth; but within that world there is hierarchy of Brahman families some of whom are sacred in relation to others. Every woman though congenitally impure, is sacred to all adult men; if she is pregnant, she also becomes sacred to all other women of the tribe except her close relatives; and these other women constitute in relation to her a profane world, which at that moment includes all children and adult men. . . . Thus the "magic circles" pivot, shifting as a person moves from one place in society to another. The categories and concepts which embody them operate in such a way that whoever passes through the various positions of a lifetime one day sees the sacred where before he has seen the profane, or vice versa.[26]

One form of the sacred within a society can clash with another. What happens when two sacred principles demand our allegiance and only one can be realized? The tension between social and individual integrity is a perennial conflict between two forms of honor, and ultimately two forms of sacredness.

We have arrived at the important idea of the relativity of the sacred not only *among* different worlds but even *within* one. What is right, clean, or fitting at one time and stage may well be wrong, dirty, or unfitting at another. Impurity will be relative to expectations. The child cannot be impure in the way an adult can. The mystic and priest have standards of purity that are beyond the layperson. We have seen how Buddhism kept evolving new contexts and standards of enlightenment.

To become holy is to become free of impurity. But what kind of impurity? And free in relation to what ultimate standard? What emptiness? What god? What myth?

The thematic investigation of the pure/impure pattern opens up a large and important range of religious phenomena not revealed by other comparative categories. Purity is not just the fear of pollution but a function of the unity and integrity of the world. Purity may have any content, may take expression in both external and internal realms, and may pivot historically and socially. Every culture fills it with new values. Once you are familiar with the theme, religious practice takes on a new relevance as data for such questions as: How is a world divided? Within any given system, what is it that constitutes purity or holiness? What requirements does the goal of the system place on the conduct of individual and community? What opposes the sacred, and how is profanity dealt with or transformed? Neither religious history nor the study of religious history have yet exhausted the possible variations on these themes.

8

Comparative Perspective: Some Concluding Points

WE have seen what unfolds when religion is viewed not only as a set of different traditions but as typical forms of expression present in all traditions. Elucidating these forms provides a framework for understanding how religious worlds are composed and provides a way of doing justice to both the common structure and the indulgent variety of religion. What may we now conclude about the general nature and implications of such comparative study?

The Comparative Process

Religious expressions are manifestations of more than their own singular, historical context; they are also special embodiments of the ongoing, human activity of world fashioning. History continually re-creates the world in new and different settings. Any particular mythic expression shows anew the force and function of mythic language, mythic origins, and mythic prototypes. Any particular god shows one more possibility of the sort of thing a god can be, the sort of realm a god can govern. Any rite, any sacred time, embodies the

161

expressive and renewing power of ritual focus. Any distinction of pure and impure, sacred and profane, right and wrong, shows the perennial process of differentiating and mediating oppositions, choosing paths, and following disciplines. In this way each version of myth, god, rite, or path gains a certain intelligibility through its connectedness with a thematic history; and to that history, to the repertoire of that theme, each religious expression adds its own specific contribution.

Through the cumulative nature of comparative study, religious history becomes increasingly resonant with thematic material. Comparative perspective is built up over time. It compounds associations. It brings more and more analogies and typological contexts to bear in its reading of history and behavior. Knowledge of each religious system contributes to our understanding of the next, and each "new" religious expression has the advantage of being viewed in relation to things that are like it in some ways and different in others. In music, the trained ear hears more structure but also more difference, more detail, and it inevitably hears every new instance of music within the overall context of the history of musical expression. It is the same with religion. Comparative perspective is educated perspective.

Like the educational process itself, comparative work must respect the real interplay, and not just the imagined interplay, of structure and diversity. Neither analogy nor difference should be avoided, and any preemptive overweighting of the one or the other might be suspected of ideological defensiveness. True comparative sensibility is held captive neither by particulars nor universals, neither by the sheer variety of history nor by hang-on-to-them-at-all-costs generalizations. Certainly the complexity of real history is a constant challenge to any typology. While acquiring a seasoned sense of the relative importance of structure and fact, the comparativist must see that, if the information delivered by the particular occasion doesn't fit the patterns of the viewing lens, the lens should be changed. Where concepts of myth and ritual serve no illuminating purpose, drop them.

In this study we have focused on the synchronic, cross-cultural dimension of comparison and have done little with the use of comparison in strictly diachronic, historical analysis.

All the more reason to remember here that understanding a world involves not just global perspective but the detailed study of that world's own particular history. As one historian of religion puts it, "Knowing what a given group has to say about its life by itself does not help us to make sense of what the group wishes to say. It is only in discovering the choices, the contexts in which statements are made . . . that the statements begin to make sense."[1] This, then, is the historical side of the matter: the study of the "comparative" choices that religious life makes *within* the horizon of a particular world. Historical and thematic contexts are different yet nonconflicting levels of analysis. The first tries to reconstruct what things actually mean or meant to adherents. The second utilizes the perspective of the *whole set* of historical religious worlds in order to illumine the religiously generic facets of any particular world. This broader, thematic perspective of comparative study need not obliterate or obscure the process of understanding what things mean to the religious insider.

Categories such as world, myth, ritual time, gods, and purity are justified if they enhance our understanding of religious life or (and this is not insignificant) help us avoid *mis*understanding religious life. They are working categories to be explored and tested through historical or field study. They comprise not so much a theory about the nature of man but a set of orientational concepts that can lend a certain thematic intelligibility to otherwise opaque historical and behavioral phenomena. They are not timeless patterns of meaning that imply that everything is the same or means the same thing, but ways of discerning analogies of structure. The categories of this book are but operational guides to a territory that in other times and cultures will be thematized in different ways, according to different conceptual needs.

It is also a hypothesis of this study that these structures of religion have a common, theoretical cohesiveness. They all illustrate the process of world definition. The referent of religious study here is therefore not some transcendental, mysterious reality that one has to believe in intuitively in order for the whole comparative enterprise to make sense. The common referent is "world." Myth, with its images of origins and endings, and with its grounding paradigms and stories, presents the very foundation of an inhabited universe. Gods crystallize how we address and are addressed by those agencies on which our world depends. Ritual, with its times for all seasons, monitors all that is of enduring worth and all that changes in life, linking the human microcosm with the abiding symbols and order of the larger cosmos. Religious disciplines create paths in the midst of chaos, separating the undifferentiated world into zones of order and disorder, positive and negative choices, realms of integrity and pollution. So these patterns of comparative study are not Platonic archetypes that exist in an independent, timeless realm, but are rather the active, channeling, typical ways that religions create worlds. World is what they are about, what they pattern. And this is why the whole comparative religion endeavor can be of such rich interest; religious systems, as a set, represent far-reaching questions about the relative, locational nature of that thing that fascinates us all, the world. The subject matter is not trivial.

Some would want to say that what religion is about is not the world but God, or the supernatural. Yet as used here the idea of world *contains* the idea of divinity and all the other things that humans have taken as real. Religious people experience the world *as* a place created by God or *as* a manifestation of Brahman. So there is mystery enough in the term *world* if what a world can be in fact *includes* everything humans have ever experienced it to be. In the eyes of the religious perceiver, there is no limit to what the world can be. The comparative enterprise, unavoidably, is a journey into the lessons of such possibility and relativity.

The Comparative Mirror

The comparative study of religious worlds invites self-reflection about the nature of our own cultural systems. Comparative perspective supplies a context for the perception of our immediate world. As the anthropologist Clifford Geertz observes,

> To see ourselves as others see us can be eye-opening. To see others as sharing a nature with ourselves is the merest decency. But it is from the far more difficult achievement

of seeing ourselves amongst others, as a local example of
the forms human life has locally taken, a case among cases,
a world among worlds, that the largeness of mind, without
which objectivity is self-congratulation and tolerance a
sham, comes.[2]

If we have examined the variations on ritual time A through
Z and the worlds expressed through those variations, we will
be apt to take a keener interest in what it is that we observe
in our special occasions and times of passages. What do we
renew? What do we celebrate? Into what do we induct our
young? Our own world, instead of being taken for granted,
becomes exposed *as* a world, its contents get held up to the
comparative mirror, and we become a phenomenon to ourselves. The Eton-raised Colin Turnbull found revealing aspects
of the adolescent passage customs of British schoolboys *after*
he had lived in the Pygmy culture and observed its puberty
rites.[3]

One of the contemporary needs of Western religious studies is to bring the phenomena of biblical religions into the
comparative context, and to do so in an even-handed way.
We saw how many earlier approaches either made Christianity
the measure of all else or brought it into comparative view
only to belittle it. But biblical religion, and this includes its
contemporary, living manifestations, needs to be understood
as an integral part of the subject matter of the sacred, part of
the history of mythic language and ritual enactment. The more
we understand the comparative structures of religiousness itself, the less will we engage in superficial reactiveness to Western religions and the more richly will we be able to read the
"texts" of the myth and ritual systems all around us, including
the religious systems of our own hometown. Each religion
around us—no matter whether it finds current favor with outsiders—is a living, mythic world for its adherents, a fusion of
modern settings and traditional religious symbolism. Existence
and myth, as illustrated extensively in this book, shape each
other. If Easter is celebrated in star-conscious Hollywood with
sunrise "celebrity readings" at the Hollywood Bowl, the contemporary form of the event becomes but one more occasion
for myth to express itself through the existential categories of

culture. In an electronic age, television ministries are normal media for the gods, and the turn of a channel gives instant access to mythic language and worlds. And if theologians write and speak about the relevancy of scriptural symbols to modern life, we should recognize that this, too, is part of the history of myth.

The differences and conflicts among religious positions represent issues about mythic models. What language is to be used to name the powers that be? The coming to consciousness and critical urgency of myth is seen in many places. It has special vividness in feminist critiques of male-oriented religious symbol systems and in the call for canons and paradigms relevant to the spiritual lives of women. Rosemary Ruether explains the need behind her assembling of such a canon in *Womanguides:*

> Feminist theology cannot be done from the existing base of the Christian Bible. The Old and New Testaments have been shaped in their formation, their transmission, and, finally, their canonization, to sacralize patriarchy. . . . In their present form and intention they are designed to erase women's existence as subjects and to mention women only as objects of male definition.[4]

"New Age" religion, similarly, presents a panorama of voices and mythologies that, issuing from the wells of myth, are clear alternatives to conventional historical paradigms.

Just as the patterns that emerge in a comparative study of religious worlds allow us to see the continuity of Western monotheisms with the whole history of religious language, they also show certain thematic continuities with secular worlds. If we understand religious myth, we may gain some insight into the powerful role of origins, historical or moral prototypes, and sacred foundational principles in any culture, secular or otherwise. Ritual is clearly a universal phenomenon, and we have seen how every human world gives illustration to it. Religious concepts of pure and impure have analogies in any kind of collective or individual behavior that defines profanity, punishes violations, and regulates oppositions. The history and types of religious purity and holiness open our eyes to the element of the sacred and profane throughout all human experience.

The element of the sacred is not just a possession of traditional theistic religions. The sacred is that on which life is believed to be inviolably based, that for which one will make sacrifices, the point where one's world is ultimately at stake. It embodies and protects identity.[5] Modern, secular arenas where sacredness accrues are the symbols of the state or "the Revolution," and the sanctity of individual rights, social justice, freedom, and equality. Many contemporary public issues such as the "right to life/right to choose" question are in the final analysis issues about what is sacred. So the connection of sacredness with the foundations and boundaries of worlds continues in modern behavior, and in ways that might go beyond sociopolitical levels of analysis.

Modernity is sometimes said to be postreligious, but secular worlds are worlds nonetheless. Secular life is typically estranged from traditional myth and ritual and lacking in strong socially cohesive values. Yet the absence of rites of passage to adulthood in modern Western cultures, to take one example, might also mirror a new set of values, and not merely some sort of emptiness or absence of a world. If there are no collectively fixed values and roles that youth are inducted into, is this not partly a testimony to the starkly individualistic values and character of the culture? We might even venture that it is not so much that moderns lack rites of passage as that they have implicitly allowed the adventurous, trial-and-error individual discovery of the world and self to serve *as* that passage. The mythless ego precisely must learn on its own just what it takes to become an individual, to come to self-knowledge and self-expression, to experience freedom, to become an adult, to have a world. The chaos of the ego's adolescence—or the tribulations of the psychoanalytic patient—bear definite analogy to an initiatory ordeal.

The comparativist is rarely without a home base of some kind. He or she ventures back and forth from that base. But because of the transcultural experience, the place one returns to will never be the same as the place one left. One's own world inevitably comes to embody the thematic perspectives one has brought back.

Interpreting Relativity

The "relativity of worlds" can have a subversive ring. Some have thought that the comparative study of religion necessarily presupposes or implies a kind of cynical relativism, a denial of any absolutes or common truth. But does the concept of many worlds represent a "position" of some kind? Although this is surely a topic for another study altogether, touching on huge philosophical debates,[6] it is enough to consider a few basic distinctions here.

If the comparative approach acknowledges many worlds, it does so not to "agree" with them on the one hand or to reduce them to "merely" human projections on the other, but rather to approach the subject matter in a manner appropriate to the goals of understanding and description. The comparativist's polycentric universe is not in itself a personal or metaphysical position (although it could presumably become one) but a phenomenological premise required by the field of study. That there are many kinds of people in many kinds of locations does not necessarily imply that every religion is right, or that every religion is wrong, or that there is no common ground for agreement or disagreement. Understanding a world is one thing; making claims about it is another.

Stressing parallels in the form rather than the content of religious behavior may appear to ignore the pursuit of common and normative religious truths. Some do claim that "all the great world religions teach an ethic of love for fellow humans and respect for a supreme reality"—an approach that scans comparative material for prescriptive results. I have been content to avoid this here, not because the search for areas of agreement is unworthy or uninstructive but because it is ultimately a different type of enterprise, respectfully left for other occasions or other interpreters. For purposes of the present study, the common forms of world building *themselves* represent a significant form of human unity.

To be sure, the comparative study of religion is not just a matter of knowledge but also of capacity. It requires a certain tolerance and respect for diversity. The great outward variety of religious life—with its many conflicting worldviews and practices—must somehow be matched by a commensurate inward capacity to comprehend and understand it. This is obviously no small premise. Nor is it just an academic matter that can be taught. For those with highly specific or narrow religious commitments there is often a real difficulty here. To be open even conceptually or momentarily to what another system is saying might be felt as a violation of one's own position and allegiances.

While understanding and evaluation are two quite different activities, they are not necessarily mutually exclusive in the life of any particular interpreter. The dispassionate pursuit to understand multiple versions of the sacred is not some kind of poor substitute for possessing a religious world of one's own. Comparative work does not mean that as a human being one must exist in a state of religious paralysis, having so many choices as to stymie all sense of individual judgment and value. The relativity of worlds is a descriptive observation. What the student of worlds thinks they all add up to is a matter of individual judgment and vision.

Comparativists are apt to have any number of ways of construing diversity. For some, the heterogeneity of religious worlds suggests types of evolving consciousness.[7] For others it represents ways that divinity reveals itself, patternings of the human psyche, or simply cultural variations. For some, the many worlds hover over the void; for others they are the very stuff of the gods. Paradoxically, in even mentioning such systems of interpretation we begin to make a kind of U-turn, finding ourselves back in the subject matter of worldviews—in this case the worlds of modern interpretation—as an object of study and respect. The conceptual world we inhabit will ultimately become the frame for our interpretation of the history and variety of religion.

In spite of this circularity, the larger questions of judgment should logically follow, not precede, comparative work. Evaluation of the liabilities of religious behavior—psychopaths are "told by God" to murder—is something we cannot avoid, but it is another order of business. Like anything that involves humans, religious phenomena can be noble or degrading, archaic or sophisticated, ugly or beautiful, and so on, according to any given criteria. The previous references to "everything myth can be" or "everything a god can be," deliberately create an initial, neutral ground in order to emphasize the importance of seeing religious history as subject matter. Again, it is as though within the world of music one might speak of all the possibilities of sound, or within the world of art, all the possibilities of form, without yet needing to distinguish between "low" or "high" music or art. First things first. First understanding, then evaluation.

The very setting in which we carry out this work is itself a highly pluralistic world, a pluralism that is clearly one of the confrontive facts of modern life. Many worlds are the very stuff of our world today, and their respective mythologies are exactly and urgently what we must learn to comprehend.

The comparative study of religion, accordingly, is part of this education to diversity. It prepares us to encounter not only other centers and calendars, and numerous versions of the sacred and profane, but also to decipher and appreciate different modes of language and behavior. Toward that end the old agenda advocating knowledge about "other peoples' beliefs" played and continues to play an indispensable role. But the further, deeper, and more vital educational question now is not just "What do other people believe?" but the less parochial and more starkly modern "What sort of a thing is a religious system anyway, and how does it provide us with knowledge about ourselves and our world?"

Notes

Introduction

1. Representative of this approach are two classic works: Gerardus van der Leeuw, *Religion in Essence and Manifestation: A Study in Phenomenology,* trans. J. E. Turner (1933; New York: Harper, 1963), and Mircea Eliade, *Patterns in Comparative Religion,* trans. Rosemary Sheed (New York: Sheed and Ward, 1958; first published 1949). Exemplary introductory textbooks surveying types of religious phenomena are Frederick J. Streng, *Understanding Religious Life,* 3d ed. (Belmont, Calif.: Wadsworth Publishing Company, 1985); Ninian Smart, *Worldviews: Crosscultural Explorations of Human Beliefs* (New York: Charles Scribner's Sons, 1983); and Roger Schmidt, *Exploring Religion,* 2d ed. (Belmont, Calif.: Wadsworth Publishing Company, 1988).

2. For a sophisticated analysis of the concept of comparison through controlled analogies, see Fitz John Porter Poole, "Metaphors and Maps: Towards Comparison in the Anthropology of Religion," *Journal of the American Academy of Religion* 54, no. 3 (Fall 1986): 411–60.

3. Thomas Robbins, *A View of All Religions,* 3d ed. (Hartford, Conn.: Oliver D. Cooke & Sons, 1824), vi.

4. Robert N. Bellah, *Beyond Belief: Essays on Religion in a Post-Traditional World* (New York: Harper and Row, 1970), 21.

5. For an excellent history of the term *religion* in the West, see Wilfred Cantwell Smith, *The Meaning and End of Religion: A New Approach to the Religious Traditions of Mankind* (New York: Macmillan, 1963), chap. 2.

Chapter 1: Some Traditional
Strategies of Comparison

1. *Encyclopaedia Brittanica*, 3d ed. (London, 1796), 16:71.

2. William Laurance Brown, *A Comparative View of Christianity*, 2 vols. (Edinburgh: A. Balfour and Co., 1826), 1:172.

3. Frank E. Manuel, *The Eighteenth Century Confronts the Gods* (Cambridge, Mass.: Harvard University Press, 1959), 115. The reference is to Gerhard Croese's *Homeros Hebraios* (1704).

4. George Faber, *The Origin of Pagan Idolatry Ascertained from Historical Testimony and Circumstantial Evidence*, 3 vols. (London: Rivington, 1816).

5. For this point and a selection from Faber, see the useful anthology of Burton Feldman and Robert D. Richardson, *The Rise of Modern Mythology: 1680–1860* (Bloomington: Indiana University Press, 1975), 397–407.

6. A quote from the eighteenth-century Christian Patrick Delaney, cited in David Pailin, *Attitudes to Other Religions: Comparative Religion in Seventeenth- and Eighteenth-Century Britain* (Manchester: Manchester University Press, 1984), 36.

7. Manuel, *Eighteenth Century*, 115.

8. Father Joseph François Lafitau, *Customs of the American Indians Compared with the Customs of Primitive Times*, ed. and trans. William N. Fenton and Elizabeth L. Moore (Toronto: Champlain Society, 1974), 1:280.

9. Alexander Ross, *Mystagogus Poeticus, Or the Muses Interpreter* (1648; reprint, New York: Garland Publishing Co., 1976), 3.

10. Ibid., 25.

11. Charles Blount, *Anima Mundi: or, An Historical Narration of the Opinions of the Ancients Concerning Man's Soul after This Life*, in *Miscellaneous Works* (London, 1695), 11–12. Cited in Pailin, *Attitudes*, 14.

12. For this and traditional Christian treatments of Islam, see Pailin, *Attitudes*, 81–104.

13. Alexander Ross, *Pansebeia, or a View of all the Religions of the World*, 6th ed. (London: Gillyflower and Freeman, 1696), 381.

14. My summary is from James Freeman Clarke, *Ten Great Religions: An Essay in Comparative Theology*, 24th ed. (Boston: Houghton, Mifflin & Co., 1887).

15. Particularly the Gospel of John 1:1, 14.

16. See "Declaration on the Relationship of the Church to Non-Christian Religions," *The Documents of Vatican II*, ed. Walter M. Abbott, S.J. (New York: Guild Press, 1966), 660–68. One passage in the document reads, "The Catholic Church rejects nothing which is true and holy in these religions. She looks with sincere respect upon those ways of conduct and of life, those rules and teachings which, though differing in many particulars from what she holds and sets forth, nevertheless often reflect a ray of that Truth which enlightens all men" (662).

17. For example, see John Hick and Paul F. Knitter, eds., *The Myth of Christian Uniqueness: Toward a Pluralistic Theology of Religions* (Maryknoll, N.Y.: Orbis Books, 1987), which explores a "pluralistic paradigm"; and Leonard Swidler, ed., *Toward a Universal Theology of Religion* (Maryknoll, N.Y.: Orbis Books, 1987), with contributions from eminent Christian theologians of both Protestant and Catholic faiths.

18. *Philosophical Dictionary*, trans. and ed. P. Gay (New York: Harcourt, Brace & World, 1962), 215. Cited in Pailin, *Attitudes*, 58.

19. David Hume, *The Natural History of Religion, and Dialogues Concerning Natural Religion*, ed. A. Wayne Colver and John Waldimir Price (Oxford: Clarendon Press, 1976), 61–62.

20. Ibid., 69.

21. James G. Frazer, "Preface to the Second Edition," in *The Golden Bough: A Study in Magic and Religion*, reprint of the 3d ed. (New York: St. Martin's Press, 1966), 1:xxvi.

22. Viscount Amberley [John Russell], *An Analysis of Religious Belief* (New York: D. M. Bennett, 1877; New York: Arno Press, 1972), 646.

23. Ibid.

24. Sigmund Freud, *The Future of an Illusion*, trans. W. D. Robson-Scott, rev. and ed. James Strachey (New York: Doubleday, 1964), 63. (Original edition, 1927.)

25. The theory of Louis M. Langles, cited in Manuel, *Eighteenth Century*, 114.

26. *The Gospel of Sri Ramakrishna*, trans. Swami Nikhilananda, abridged ed. (New York: Ramakrishna-Vivekananda Center, 1958), 60–61.

27. Joseph Campbell, *The Hero with a Thousand Faces*, Bollingen Series, no. 17 (Princeton, N.J.: Princeton University Press, 1949).

Chapter 2: Religion as a Subject Matter

1. For general works on the history of the modern study of religion, see Eric Sharpe, *Comparative Religion: A History*, 2d ed., (La Salle, Ill.: Open Court, 1986), and Jacques Waardenburg, *Classical Approaches to the Study of Religion*, vol. 1 (The Hague: Mouton, 1973).

2. As a young orientalist, Müller came from Germany to Oxford in 1846 and spent the remainder of his life there.

3. F. Max Müller, *Lectures on the Science of Religion* (New York: Charles Scribner & Co., 1872), 102.

4. Ibid., 6.

5. Hannah Adams, *A View of Religions*, 3d ed. (Boston: Manning and Loring, 1801), vii.

6. Müller, *Lectures*, 10–11.

7. "Preface to the Second Edition," *The Golden Bough: A Study in Magic and Religion*, reprint of 3d ed. (New York: St. Martin's Press, 1966), 1:xxvi.

8. Edward Caird, *The Evolution of Religion*, 2d ed. (Glasgow: James Maclehouse & Sons, 1894), 1.

9. See especially the often-cited methodological statements in Gerardus van der Leeuw, *Religion in Essence and Manifestation: A Study in Phenomenology*, trans. J. E. Turner (1933; New York: Harper, 1963), chaps. 107–110.

10. The Rumanian-born Eliade taught at the University of Chicago from 1956 to his death in 1986. A good introduction to his basic ideas is *The Sacred and the Profane: The Nature of Religion*, trans. Willard R. Trask (New York: Harcourt Brace Jovanovich, 1959). For statements of his overall vision for the field, see *The Quest: History and Meaning in Religion* (Chicago: University of Chicago Press, 1969), chaps. 1 and 4.

11. P. D. Chantepie de la Saussaye, *Manual of the Science of Religion*, trans. (from German) Beatrice S. Colyer-Fergusson (London: Longmans, Green & Co., 1891).

12. W. Robertson Smith, *The Religion of the Semites: The Fundamental Institutions*, 2d ed. (New York: Meridian Books, 1956). (Originally published, 1889.)

13. Frank Manuel, *The Changing of the Gods* (Hanover, N.H.: University Press of New England, 1983), 166.

14. For example, Jacques Waardenburg has called for a "new style" phenomenology that is not focused on comparative forms but on the world of religious participants. His model is living rather than extinct religions. See his *Reflections on the Study of Religion*, Religion and Reason Series, no. 15 (The Hague: Mouton, 1978). Another good analysis of the contextualist implications of phenomenology is Evan M. Zuesse, "The Role of Intentionality in the Phenomenology of Religion," in *Journal of the American Academy of Religion* 53, no. 1 (March 1985): 51–74.

15. See especially Wilfred Cantwell Smith, *The Meaning and End of Religion: A New Approach to the Religious Traditions of Mankind* (New York: Macmillan, 1963). The work is a sustained critique of the way the concept "religion" gets in the way of understanding the religious worlds of others.

16. Müller, *Lectures*, 103.

17. *Mana*, the Melanesian word for supernatural power, was taken by many scholars as a suitable generic term for the mysterious, sacred force acknowledged in most religious systems. See R. R. Marett, *The Threshold of Religion* (London: Methuen & Co., 1909), for a theory of religion that made mana—and its "negative" correlate, taboo—central.

18. Rudolf Otto, *The Idea of the Holy: An Inquiry into the Non-Rational Factor in the Idea of the Divine and its Relation to the Rational*, trans. (from German) John W. Harvey (New York: Oxford University Press, 1958). (Originally published, 1917.)

19. Emile Durkheim, *The Elementary Forms of the Religious Life*, trans. (from French) Joseph W. Swain (New York: Free Press, 1965). (First published, 1912.)

20. For a review of contributions to the study of religion after 1945, see Frank Whaling, ed., *Contemporary Approaches to the Study of Religion*, 2 vols. (Berlin: Mouton, 1984, 1985). The brilliant and provocative writings of Jonathan Z. Smith are a good example of current work that joins scholarship in religion with theoretical activity in other humanities and social sciences. See his *Map Is Not Territory: Studies in the History of Religions* (Leiden: Brill, 1978); *Imagining Religion: From Babylon to Jonestown* (Chicago: University of Chicago Press, 1982); and *To Take Place: Toward Theory in Ritual* (Chicago: University of Chicago Press, 1987). Charles H. Long's *Significations: Signs, Symbols, and Images in the Interpretation of Religion* (Philadelphia: Fortress Press, 1986) is a fine collection of suggestive essays by a leading phenomenologist of religion.

Chapter 3: Worlds

1. For an accessible work dealing with the concept of world and its relation to religion, see Peter L. Berger, *The Sacred Canopy: Elements of a Sociological Theory of Religion* (New York: Doubleday, 1967).

2. *World* derives from the Old English *wer*, man, and *yldo*, age.

3. The best example is Ernst Cassirer (1874–1945), in *The Philosophy of Symbolic Forms*, 3 vols., trans. Ralph Manheim (New Haven, Conn.: Yale University Press, 1955). To Cassirer, for instance, mythic language is not "about" a world of given objects but itself first produces those objects: "All theoretical cognition takes its departure from a world already preformed by language; the scientist, the historian, even the philosopher, lives with his objects only as language presents them to him" [*Language and Myth*, trans. Susanne K. Langer (New York: Dover Publications, 1953), 28]. A useful work relating the insights of the most influential philosopher of language, Ludwig Wittgenstein, to the study of social worlds is David Bloor, *Wittgenstein: A Social Theory of Knowledge* (New York: Columbia University Press, 1983). For a substantive review of cognitive models (for conceptualizing the world), writing within the new field of "cognitive science," see George Lakoff, *Women, Fire, and Dangerous Things: What Categories Reveal about the Mind* (Chicago: University of Chicago Press, 1987).

4. See Maurice Merleau-Ponty, *The Phenomenology of Perception*, trans. Colin Smith (New York: Humanities Press, 1962), and Maurice Natanson, *Edmund Husserl: Philosopher of Infinite Tasks* (Evanston, Ill.: Northwestern University Press, 1973). Martin Heidegger's analysis of place in terms of "dwelling," as opposed to merely "occupying," is relevant here, too. See his *Poetry, Language, Thought*, trans. Albert Hofstadter (New York: Harper and Row, 1971), part 4. For an application of phenomenology to sociology, see Peter L. Berger and Thomas Luckmann, *The Social Construction of Reality: A Treatise in the Sociology of Knowledge* (Garden City, N.Y.: Doubleday, 1966).

5. The writings of Michel Foucault (1926–1985) have been especially provocative and influential in this regard.

6. This is a central point of the analysis of Peter Berger, *The Sacred Canopy*, chap. 2.

7. A good selection of Max Weber's thought is found in *The Sociology of Religion*, trans. Ephraim Fischoff (Boston: Beacon Press, 1963).

8. Representative works are Nancy A. Falk and Rita M. Gross, eds., *Unspoken Worlds: Women's Religious Lives in Non-Western Cultures* (New York: Harper and Row, 1980); Caroline Walker Bynum, Stevan Harrell, and Paula Richman, eds., *Gender and Religion: On the Complexity of Symbols* (Boston: Beacon Press, 1986); and Arvind Sharma, ed., *Women in World Religions* (Albany: State University of New York Press, 1987).

9. For a discussion of the difference between the intimate power of particular local or "loric" places and universal, sacred authority—a distinction between "place" and "world"—see Walter L. Brenneman, Jr., and Stanley O. Yarian, *The Seeing Eye: Hermeneutical Phenomenology in the Study of Religion* (University Park: Pennsylvania State University Press, 1982), ch. 8.

10. Jonathan Z. Smith develops the point that one is threatened not so much by the distant "other" but by the "proximate" other because it is here in intersystem feuds and invasions that one's authority and territory is most acutely disputed. See Smith's "What a Difference a Difference Makes," in *"To See Ourselves as Others See Us": Christians, Jews, and "Others" in Late Antiquity,* ed. Jacob Neusner and Ernest S. Frerichs (Chico, Calif.: Scholars Press, 1985).

11. For an incisive account of this factor in the confrontation of Europeans and Indians in "the New World," see Tsvetan Todorov, *The Conquest of America: The Question of the Other* (New York: Harper and Row, 1984).

12. See Jacob Needleman and George Baker, eds., *Understanding the New Religions* (New York: Seabury Press, 1978).

13. Notable studies are Robert S. Ellwood and Harry B. Partin, *Religious and Spiritual Groups in Modern America,* 2d ed. (Englewood Cliffs, N.J.: Prentice-Hall, 1988, and H. Neill McFarland, *The Rush Hour of the Gods: A Study of New Religious Movements in Japan* (New York: Harper and Row, 1967).

14. Notable examples are Margot Adler, *Drawing Down the Moon: Witches, Druids, Goddess-Worshippers, and Other Pagans in America Today,* rev. ed. (Boston: Beacon Press, 1987), and Starhawk, *The Spiral Dance: A Rebirth of the Ancient Religion of the Great Goddess* (San Francisco: Harper and Row, 1979).

15. Robert N. Bellah, Richard Madsen, William M. Sullivan, Ann Swidler, and Steven M. Tipton, *Habits of the Heart: Individualism and Commitment in American Life* (New York: Harper and Row, 1985), 220–21.

Chapter 4: Myth

1. A good review of these interpretations of the word *myth* is William G. Doty, *Mythography: The Study of Myths and Rituals* (University: University of Alabama Press, 1986).

2. Erich Kahler, *Out of the Labyrinth: Essays in Clarification* (New York: George Braziller, 1967), 42.

3. Such writers as Friedrich Schlegel (1772–1829) and Friedrich Schelling (1775–1854) wrote influential works on the notion of myth as a universal human language and as a creative form of symbolism that was the voice and medium for shaping spiritual truths.

4. The New Testament condemns "myths" as so many "fables" (1 Timothy 1:4), "fictitious tales" (2 Peter 1:16), "old wives's tales" (1 Timothy 4:7), and "commandments of men," incompatible with the truth (2 Timothy 4:4; Titus 1:14).

5. Bronislaw Malinowski, *Magic, Science and Religion* (New York: Doubleday, 1948), 100. (Originally published in the essay, "Myth in Primitive Psychology" [1926].)

6. Kees Bolle, in *Encyclopaedia Britannica*, 15th ed. (1974), (Macropaedia), S. V. "myth and mythology," 12:794.

7. In the approach of C. G. Jung and his circle, myths and symbols are read as representing archetypes of the collective unconscious. Much can be learned about myth from these studies. But in this book I am not trying to deal with a universal psychological history of the subject but to show how mythic language works within its own worlds. That the global storehouse of myth can provide a certain contemporary self-understanding is shown in Joseph Campbell's deservedly popular book, *The Hero with a Thousand Faces*, Bollingen Series, no. 17 (Princeton, N.J.: Princeton University Press, 1949). But this phenomenon—reconstructing a kind of metamyth about the history of myths—is itself illustrative of the idea of myth as world constituting, the world here being precisely that of the modern interpreter. *Man and His Symbols*, ed. C. G. Jung et al. (New York: Dell, 1968), is a good overview of this psychological approach to myth, and Jung's autobiography, *Memories, Dreams, Reflections* (New York: Random House, 1961), is indispensable for understanding the development of his own orientation to the subject.

The structuralist approach to myth, represented by Claude Lévi-Strauss, sees myth as a language that reconciles social oppositions. There is much value in showing the detailed way in which myth contains sociocultural structures and dynamics, but structuralism does not deal with what myth means religiously in the lives of its participants.

8. John 8:58.

9. Ernst Cassirer, *The Philosophy of Symbolic Forms*, vol. 2, *Mythical Thought*, trans. Ralph Manheim (New Haven, Conn.: Yale University Press, 1955), 121.

10. Kees W. Bolle, *The Freedom of Man in Myth* (Nashville, Tenn.: Vanderbilt University Press, 1968).

11. Matthew 4:4.

12. A good treatment of the "phenomenon" of scripture and its religious function is Frederick M. Denny and Rodney L. Taylor, eds., *The Holy Book in Comparative Perspective* (Columbia: University of South Carolina Press, 1985). On the oral dimension of scripture, see William A. Graham, *Beyond the Written Word: Oral Aspects of Scripture in the History of Religion* (Cambridge: Cambridge University Press, 1987).

13. Matthew 19:6.

14. G. Reichel-Dolmatoff, *Beyond the Milky Way: Hallucinatory Imagery of the Tukano Indians* (Los Angeles: UCLA Publications, 1976), 4.

15. Excellent anthologies of cosmogonic myths are Charles H. Long, *Alpha: The Myths of Creation* (New York: Braziller, 1963), and Barbara C. Sproul, *Primal Myths: Creating the World* (New York: Harper and Row, 1979).

16. Charles F. Keyes, "Ambiguous Gender: Male Initiation in a Northern Thai Buddhist Society," in Caroline Walker Bynum et al., eds., *Gender and Religion: On the Complexity of Symbols* (Boston: Beacon Press, 1986), 75.

17. Mircea Eliade, "Myths and Mythical Thought," in Alexander Eliot, ed., *Myths* (New York: McGraw-Hill, 1976), 20.

18. Ibid., 18.

19. Cited in Huston Smith, *The Religions of Man* (New York: Harper and Row, 1965), 14–15.

20. This is one of the theses in Jonathan Z. Smith's *Imagining Religion: From Babylon to Jonestown* (Chicago: University of Chicago Press, 1982), 36–52.

21. An excellent account of this is Michael Fishbane, "The Teacher and the Hermeneutical Task: A Reinterpretation of Medieval Exegesis," *Journal of the American Academy of Religion* 43, no. 4 (December 1975): 709–21.

22. John Bierhorst, *The Mythology of North America* (New York: William Morrow & Co., 1985), 80–82.

Chapter 5: Ritual and Time

1. A fine work on ritual observance is Victor Turner, ed., *Celebration: Studies in Festivity and Ritual* (Washington, D.C.: Smithsonian Institution Press, 1982). On the state of "ritual studies" today, see Ronald L. Grimes, *Research in Ritual Studies: A Programmatic Essay and Bibliography*, ATLA Bibliography Series, no. 14 (Metuchen, N.J.: Scarecrow Press, 1985).

2. Frederick Mathewson Denny, *An Introduction to Islam* (New York: Macmillan, 1985), 345.

3. Ernst Cassirer notes, "The Latin term for pure theoretical thought and vision, *contemplari*, goes back to the idea of *templum*, the marked-off space in which the augur carried on his observations of the heavens" (*The Philosophy of Symbolic Forms*, vol. 2, *Mythical Thought*, trans. Ralph Manheim (New Haven, Conn.: Yale University Press, 1955), 102.

4. Mircea Eliade, *The Sacred and the Profane: The Nature of Religion*, trans. Willard R. Trask (New York: Harcourt, Brace, Jovanovich, 1959), 73.

5. The best description of this is in Roger Caillois, *Man and the Sacred*, trans. Meyer Barash (Glencoe, Ill.: Free Press, 1959).

6. I have included examples of "secular" and national observances in this study not only because they illustrate the character of ritual, but because there are elements of the sacred present in them. We have seen that the sacred is not limited to the notion of divinity but is a function of the attitude and world of the participants. For a fine study along these lines of the expressive nature of political ritual, past and present, see David I. Kertzer, *Ritual, Politics, and Power* (New Haven, Conn.: Yale University Press, 1988).

7. Melford E. Spiro, *Buddhism and Society: A Great Tradition and Its Burmese Vicissitudes* (New York: Harper and Row, 1970), 225.

8. For Puritan observances, see Charles E. Hambrick-Stowe, *The Practice of Piety: Puritan Devotional Disciplines in Seventeenth-Century New England* (Chapel Hill: University of North Carolina Press, 1982), ch. 4.

9. For a fuller description of these Chinese rites, see Wolfram Eberhard, *Chinese Festivals* (London: Abelard-Schuman, 1958).

10. Abraham Joshua Heschel, *The Sabbath: Its Meaning for Modern Man* (New York: Farrar, Straus, and Giroux, 1951), 8–10.

11. Hambrick-Stowe, *The Practice of Piety*, 99.

12. The phrase *rites of passage* was coined in 1908 by the French anthropologist Arnold van Gennep in his still-classic *Rites of Passage*, trans. Monika B. Vizedom and Gabrielle L. Caffee (Chicago: University of Chicago Press, 1960).

13. Gregory Bateson, *Naven*, 2d ed. (Stanford, Calif.: Stanford University Press, 1958), 7.

14. Ibid., 6.

15. J. V. Blumenthal, "Karimojong Cluster: Uganda," in *Peoples of the Earth*, vol. 2, *Africa* (Verona, Italy: Danbury Press, 1973), 124.

16. Denny, *Introduction*, 296. Denny notes that this is done in imitation of Muhammad, who is reported to have performed it on the occasion of the birth of his grandson Hasan.

17. John S. Mbiti, *African Religions and Philosophy* (Garden City, N.Y.: Doubleday, 1970), 151.

18. On this, see Mircea Eliade, *Rites and Symbols of Initiation*, trans. Willard R. Trask (New York: Harper and Row, 1965), and also Mircea Eliade, *Shamanism: Archaic Techniques of Ecstasy*, Bollingen Series, no. 76, trans. Willard R. Trask (Princeton, N.J.: Princeton University Press, 1972).

19. Christopher A. P. Binns, "The Changing Face of Power: Revolution and Accommodation in the Development of the Soviet Ceremonial System: Part II," in *Man*, N. S., 15, no. 1 (March 1980): 174–75. In this article, and in "Part I" (published in the same journal in December 1979), Binns shows the pervasiveness of ceremonies in the Soviet Union under the administration of official government agencies for "rites and festivals" that handle both calendrical and life-cycle occasions. Throughout the country there are Wedding Palaces, Palaces of the Newly Born, and Houses of Mourning. For a full study of the Lenin cult, see Nina Tumarkin, *Lenin Lives! The Lenin Cult in Soviet Russia* (Cambridge, Mass.: Harvard University Press, 1983).

20. Denny, *Introduction*, 298.

21. Spiro, *Buddhism*, 234–35.

22. Types and illustrations of modern adult passages are also the subject of Gail Sheehy's richly documented best-seller *Passages: Predictable Crises of Adult Life* (New York: Dutton, 1976).

23. John Smith, *A Map of Virginia, With a Description of the Country, the Commodities, People, Government and Religion* (Oxford: Joseph Barnes, 1612), 31. [Cited from the reprint edition in *The English Experience*, vol. 557 (New York: Da Capo Press, 1973).]

24. James M. Freeman, "The Ladies of Lord Krishna: Rituals of Middle-Aged Women in Eastern India," in *Unspoken Worlds: Women's Religious Lives in Non-Western Cultures*, ed. Nancy A. Falk and Rita M. Gross (New York: Harper & Row, 1980), 110–26.

25. Arthur Waley, "Introduction," *The Analects of Confucius*, trans. and ed. Arthur Waley (New York: Random House, n.d.), 64.

Chapter 6: Gods

1. The prototypes of the presumed root *gheu* seem to be the Sanskrit *hū*, "to invoke," or *hutâ*, "what is worshipped by sacrifice."

2. 1 Kings 20.

3. W. Brede Kristensen, *The Meaning of Religion: Lectures in the Phenomenology of Religion*, trans. John B. Carman (The Hague: Martinus Nijhoff, 1960), 146.

4. Gerardus van der Leeuw, *Religion in Essence and Manifestation: A Study in Phenomenology*, trans. J. E. Turner (1933; New York: Harper, 1963), 153.

5. Kristensen, *Meaning of Religion*, 147.

6. Ibid., 149.

7. Ibid., 147.

8. Victor Barnouw, *An Introduction to Anthropology*, vol. 2 (Homewood, Ill.: Dorsey Press, 1971), 225.

9. *The Song of God: Bhagavad-Gita*, trans. Swami Prabhavananda and Christopher Isherwood (New York: New American Library, 1972), 81–82 (chap. 9).

10. Job 38–41, from *The New Oxford Annotated Bible* (rev. standard version), ed. Herbert G. May and Bruce M. Metzger (New York: Oxford University Press, 1977).

11. For a survey of some modern guru figures, see Marvin Henry Harper, *Gurus, Swamis, and Avatars: Spiritual Masters and Their American Disciples* (Philadelphia: Westminster Press, 1972).

12. John 14:6.

13. Matthew 25:35–36.

14. See Erika Bourguignon, *Possession* (San Francisco: Chandler and Sharp, 1974), or I. M. Lewis, *Ecstatic Religion: An Anthropological Study of Spirit Possession and Shamanism* (Harmondsworth, Eng.: Penguin Books, 1971).

15. Diana L. Eck, *Darshan: Seeing the Divine Image in India* (Chambersburg, Pa.: Anima Books, 1981), 1–5.

16. For example, the Russian *bog* means giver or sharer; and the Hindu *bhagavan* is from *bhaj*, dispenser.

17. *God's Plot: The Paradoxes of Puritan Piety, Being the Autobiography and Journal of Thomas Shepard,* ed. Michael McGiffert (Amherst: University of Massachusetts Press, 1972), 72–74.

18. Micah 6:8.

19. Mircea Eliade, *Shamanism: Archaic Techniques of Ecstasy,* Bollingen Series, no. 76, trans. Willard R. Trask (Princeton, N.J.: Princeton University Press, 1972), 295–96.

20. Van der Leeuw, *Religion in Essence and Manifestation,* 351.

Chapter 7: Systems of Purity

1. An excellent textbook with a comparative approach to religious ethics is now available: David Chidester, *Patterns of Action: Religion and Ethics in Comparative Perspective* (Belmont, Calif.: Wadsworth Publishing Co., 1987). Chidester breaks new ground in bringing the study of religious conduct into the framework of the general history of religions, and thereby showing the important relationship of ethical conduct and issues to myth, ritual, and the factor of the sacred. A now classic work on mythological metaphors for purity and pollution is Paul Ricoeur's *The Symbolism of Evil,* trans. Emerson Buchanan (Boston: Beacon Press, 1967). A useful collection of essays on the different cultural meanings of evil is David Parkin, ed., *The Anthropology of Evil* (Oxford: Basil Blackwell, 1985).

2. W. Robertson Smith and James Frazer believed they had discovered a universal category in the Oceanic phenomenon of taboo and had some interesting Victorian things to say about the evolution of the idea of purity from savage ritual to civilized moral life. But it was the work of Emile Durkheim and his school that established the broader functional importance of interdictions. For a history of the anthropological use of the concept of taboo, see Franz Steiner, *Taboo* (New York: Philosophical Library, 1956).

3. See Mary Douglas's classic, *Purity and Danger: An Analysis of Concepts of Pollution and Taboo* (London: Routledge and Kegan Paul, 1966).

4. Ibid., 35.

5. *The Dhammapada*, trans. S. Radhakrishnan (Oxford: Oxford University Press, 1966), 137.

6. Douglas, *Purity and Danger*, 41–55; and Mary Douglas, *Implicit Meanings: Essays in Anthropology* (London: Routledge and Kegan Paul, 1975), 269.

7. Leviticus 20:24–26.

8. Ayatollah Sayyed Ruhollah Mousari Khomeini, *A Clarification of Questions*, trans. J. Borujerdi (Boulder, Colo.: Westview Press, 1984), 212.

9. For a development of this point, see Howard Eilberg-Schwartz, "Creation and Classification in Judaism: From Priestly to Rabbinic Conceptions," *History of Religions* 28, no. 4 (May 1987): 357–81.

10. Matthew 23:27.

11. *The Dhammapada*, 180.

12. Mark 7:15.

13. John Cassian, *The First Conference of Abbot Moses*, section 22, in *The Works of John Cassian*, trans. Edgar C. S. Gibson, in *Nicene and Post-Nicene Fathers*, ed. P. Schaff and H. Wace, vol. 11 (New York: Christian Literature Society, 1894), 307.

14. This point is developed in William E. Paden, "Theaters of Humility and Suspicion: Desert Saints and New England Puritans," in Luther H. Martin, Huck Gutman, and Patrick Hutton, eds., *Technologies of the Self: A Seminar with Michel Foucault* (Amherst: University of Massachusetts Press, 1988), 64–79.

15. Sacvan Bercovitch, *The Puritan Origins of the American Self* (New Haven, Conn.: Yale University Press, 1975), 18.

16. Thomas Shepard, in *The Works of Thomas Shepard*, vol. I (New York: AMS Press, 1967), 23.

17. Max Weber, *The Sociology of Religion*, trans. Ephraim Fischoff (Boston: Beacon Press, 1967), 166–83.

18. The social structure and paradoxes of the Indian ideals of purity are described in Louis Dumont's *Homo Hierarchicus: The Caste System and Its Implications*, trans. M. Sainsbury (London: Weidenfeld and Nicolson, 1970).

19. Bhadantacariya Buddhaghosa, *The Path of Purification,* trans. Bhikkhu Nanamoli (Colombo: R. Semage, 1956), 2.

20. *The Song of God: Bhagavad-Gita,* trans. Swami Prabhavananda and Christopher Isherwood (New York: New American Library, 1972), 58 (ch. 5).

21. K. Kavanaugh, "Purification, Spiritual," in *New Catholic Encyclopedia,* Vol. XI, p. 1042.

22. Romans 14:14; Titus 1:15.

23. *Purity and Danger,* 169–70.

24. *The Song of God: Bhagavad-Gita,* 43 (ch. 2).

25. Paul Reps, *Zen Flesh, Zen Bones: A Collection of Zen and Pre-Zen Writings* (Garden City, N.Y.: Doubleday, n.d.), 18.

26. Arnold van Gennep, *Rites of Passage,* trans. Monika B. Vizedom and Gabrielle L. Caffee (Chicago: University of Chicago Press, 1960), 12–13.

Chapter 8: Comparative Perspective: Some Concluding Points

1. Jacob Neusner, "Alike and Not Alike: A Grid for Comparison and Differentiation," in *Take Judaism, For Example,* ed. Jacob Neusner (Chicago: University of Chicago Press, 1983), 234.

2. Clifford Geertz, *Local Knowledge: Further Essays in Interpretive Anthropology* (New York: Basic Books, 1983), 16.

3. Colin Turnbull, *The Human Cycle* (New York: Simon and Schuster, 1983).

4. Rosemary Radford Ruether, *Womanguides: Readings toward a Feminist Theology* (Boston: Beacon Press, 1985), ix.

5. For a systematic, sociological analysis of the relation between "sacralization" and "identity," see Hans Mol, *Identity and the Sacred: A Sketch for a New Social-Scientific Theory of Religion* (Oxford: Basil Blackwell, 1976).

6. A fine collection of essays probing the notion of relativism as a cognitive, epistemological position is Martin Hollis and Steven Lukes, eds., *Rationality and Relativism* (Cambridge, Mass.: MIT Press, 1982). Also analyzing philosophical issues in the concept of multiple worlds is Nelson Goodman's *Ways of Worldmaking* (Indianapolis, Ind.: Hackett Publishing Co., 1978).

7. For example, see Robert N. Bellah's widely read essay, "Religious Evolution," (*American Sociological Review* 29 [1964]: 358–74). This significantly reopened the "developmental" issue by proposing the idea that the increasing differentiation of self and environment formed a criterion for discerning different stages in religious evolution. Ken Wilber's *Up from Eden: A Transpersonal View of Human Evolution* (New York: Doubleday, 1981) integrates Western psychologies and Asian mysticism, finding "pre-egoic, egoic, and trans-egoic" levels of consciousness unfolding in religious history, each type of consciousness manifesting itself through a different kind of religious observance and mythic representation.

Index